The Archive of American Journalism

Lincoln Steffens

Henry Stanley

Theodore Roosevelt

Richard Harding Davis

Ida Tarbell

Ray Stannard Baker

Nellie Bly

H.L. Mencken

Ambrose Bierce

Stephen Crane

Jack London

Mark Twain

Ernest Hemingway

www.historicjournalism.com

Repor...

The Tulsa R...

Immigrants, 1...

(to co...

The Armist...

The Palmer Rai...

The Black Sox...

The Sinking of th...

Reporting:

Immigrants
1802-1931

The Archive of American Journalism
St. Paul, MN
2020

Note on Sources

All articles are complete and unabridged, with headlines, subheads and formatting that match those of the original publication. Note that minor edits have been made to correct obsolete spelling and punctuation. Students and researchers: these are "public domain" texts that can be freely copied, reproduced and distributed without permission or cost. Please credit The Archive of American Journalism as your source.

The Archive LLC
9269 Troon Court
Woodbury, MN 55125.

Article selection and original Introduction
Copyright ©2020 by Tom Streissguth
Cover Image: Mulberry Street, New York City
(Library of Congress)

ISBN: 978-0-9907137-7-7
Printed in the United States of America

Acknowledgments

For their encouragement and suggestions, sincere thanks to Mark Lerner, Gordon Hagert, Pier Gustafson, Phil Gapp, Jonathan Peacock, John Hatch, Marian Streissguth and our original founding supporters: William F. Zeman, Phil Gapp, Walter Crowley, Adele Streissguth, Richard Prosser, Abhilash Sarhadi, James McGrath Morris

Contents

Introduction
11

Timeline
13

ARTICLES

Immigration
Lancaster Intelligencer and Journal/March 24, 1802
21

Immigration from Ireland
New York Daily Herald/July 6, 1844
23

Our Country and the Future
Athens Post (Athens, TN)/October 4, 1850
24

The Chinese in California
Louisville Daily Courier/June 12, 1852
26

Chinese Immigration–What Will Be Its Effect?
Meigs County Telegraph/August 30, 1859
27

Chinese Immigration and the Cause of Free Labor
The National Era/March 24, 1859
28

The Chinese In America
The Guardian (London)/August 19, 1868
31

The Philosophy of Migration
Western Home Journal (Lawrence, KS)/September 8, 1881
33

Mongolian Immigration
Hartford Courant/May 22, 1882
36

The Germans In America
New York Times/October 9, 1883
38

Immigration
Western Home Journal (Ottawa, KS)/January 9, 1886
41

Labor Bureau Report
Weekly Commonwealth (Topeka, KS)/January 14, 1886
43

The Slaughter Continues
San Francisco Examiner/November 11, 1891
51

Crime Among The Chinese
San Francisco Examiner/March 13, 1893
56

How Whites Smoke Opium in Chinatown
San Francisco Call/August 4, 1895
62

Huntington and Schwerin Employ Washington Lobbyists to Protect the Dishonest Chinese Passenger Traffic of the Pacific Mail
San Francisco Call/April 29, 1899
72

Italian Laborers
Pacific Commercial Advertiser/August 22, 1899
81

Grave but Uncorroborated Accusations are Made Against Chief Sullivan and Captain Wittman
San Francisco Call/February 10, 1901
86

Strong Speeches to the Delegates
San Francisco Call/November 23, 1901
99

Memorial of the Exclusion Convention Addressed to the President and Congress
San Francisco Call/November 23, 1901
101

Some of the Peculiarities, Both Picturesque and Otherwise, Of Our Italian Fellow Citizens
New York Tribune/July 12, 1903
109

The South to Get Them
The Irish Standard (Minneapolis)/May 5, 1906
115

What Are Our Immigrants Worth in Dollars and Cents?
San Francisco Call/August 25, 1907
121

**Honolulu's Highways and Byways–
Among the Opium Dens of Chinatown**
Pacific Commercial Advertiser/March 16, 1908
129

Is the Famous Italian "Black Hand" Organization a Myth?
Los Angeles Herald/January 17, 1909
133

Detective Pelosino Black Hand Victim
New York Tribune/March 14, 1909
141

Chinese Slayer Eludes Officers
Los Angeles Herald/June 22, 1909
146

The Black Hand Scourge
The Daily Democrat (Anadarko, OK)/September 27, 1909
151

Reds Rush Here from Mexico
New York Sun/November 24, 1919
157

3 Hundred Reds Sail for Russia
The Brainerd Daily Dispatch (Brainerd, MN)/December 21, 1919
161

How Shall the Alien Be Made Into a Good American?
New York Tribune/April 4, 1920
163

The Problem of Immigration
Wilmington Morning News/December 28, 1920
169

How the International Rogues Greet the Immigrants
New York Herald/April 30, 1922
171

Hardships Third Class Immigrants Have to Bear At Ellis Island
The New York Times/December 17, 1922
177

Immigration Law Defended, Also Scored
Evening Journal (Wilmington, DE)/January 24, 1929
185

Farrington Attacks Stand of McClatchy
Honolulu Star-Bulletin/October 3, 1931
189

For Further Reading
199

Online Resources
203

from The Archive
204

from historicjournalism.com
206

Introduction

In colonial times there was little difference made between immigrants and Americans. There were the recently arrived, the established, and those striving to be established.

Outrage concerning immigrants in the United States began after independence, and probably well before 1802, the year of this collection's first article. The argument laid out in an anonymous letter to the *Lancaster Intelligencer* was economic: immigrants would compete for jobs and threaten the livelihoods of the citizens, whose families should enjoy the privileges that came with stepping ashore at an earlier date. It seems a self-evident argument and hard to refute, until one considers the problem of settling a continent-sized nation without immigrants to do most of the settling. Surely some balance could be struck: useful and cheap foreign labor versus job security for "natives." It was on this basis that the first immigration laws were passed in the mid-19th century.

By the 1840s, the debate took on new dimensions on ethnic, social and religious grounds. Catholic Irish fleeing starvation were considered of lesser benefit to the nation than good Protestant stock from northern Europe and England. The arrival of city-dwellers also raised an issue. Immigration opponents became concerned critics of the overcrowded, unhealthy conditions that resulted when immigrants remained in the ports of their arrival, rather than taking to the land. Hostility for the degraded eastern cities--and their politicians--on the part of the healthy and virtuous western country-dwellers dates from this era.

Various strains of anti-immigrant ideology can be further traced through newspapers of the late 19th and early 20th centuries. Dark and ominous headlines brooded over many stories of murder and gang warfare among the clannish Italians. The existence of the Black Hand, an underworld organization imported by Sicilian arrivals, was a hot subject for debate over many years. Gambling and opium brought by San Francisco's Chinese immigrants gave rise to Chinese exclusion, written into federal law in 1882. The corruption of public bureaucrats and railroad officials profiting from trade in immigrant transport and labor also made for good reads in the papers.

The sensational revelations goaded lawmakers to act: immigration laws of the 1890s and 1920s restricted new arrivals as a percentage of those already arrived from the same country. These laws were inspired by the compulsion to reset the country's social makeup to an imagined better past, well before steamship travel made the voyage to New York and other ports easy, even for the poor, for Asians, for southern Europeans.

Excluding immigrants on the basis of limited wealth arrived later. The problem, as laid out in "The Problem of Immigration" and other articles of the 1920s, was simply one of cost and benefit. The poor, in this view, were naturally less desirable than the rich, on the basis that they were more likely to become a "public charge." This ignored the fact that the rich also posed their costs to the public finances--and the poor were required to pay taxes that supported them, like anybody else.

The menace of undesirable political views was another major theme of immigration stories in the years after World War I. Russians in this era were associated with anarchists and Communists, and socialism provided grounds for deportation, no matter the raised lamp before the land of liberty and the promise of breathing free. The newspapers were, by and large, glad to see them go, and had little argument with the government's often-violent enforcement of right Americanism and political correctness.

The familiar arguments are startlingly revealed in these columns, letters and stories. They're still raging today, as sternly as they were in the past. It's a common sense view that there would be no United States of the present, or future, without immigrants--but it seems the country never will agree on who to admit, who to exclude, or how to arrive at that important decision.

Timeline

1790
The Naturalization Act of 1790 allows any free white person of "good character," who has been living in the United States for two years or longer to apply for citizenship. Candidates must swear allegiance to the Constitution; children under 21 of naturalized citizens also become citizens.

The first U.S. census counts 3.9 million people in the United States, with English as the largest ethnic group.

1798
By the Alien and Sedition Acts, noncitizens must have lived in the United States for 14 years before becoming citizens. Anyone deemed "dangerous to the peace and safety of the United States" may be deported.

1815
The Treaty of Ghent ends the War of 1812 between England and the United States. A wave of European immigration begins; one-third of immigrants between 1820 and 1860 will come from Ireland, while 5 million Germans will also arrive.

1819
The Steerage Act of 1819 requires shipping companies to improve conditions for passengers carried across the Atlantic from Europe. Ship captains are also required to submit records of immigrant origins.

1849
Opponents of Catholic immigration from Europe join the growing Know Nothing movement, which forms the American party in 1855.

1850s

Immigrants from China begin arriving on the the west coast to work in mining, garment manufacturing, railroad construction, and agriculture.

1864

By the Immigration Act, the Congress establishes the office of Commissioner of Immigration. Labor contracts made outside the United States are deemed enforceable in US courts.

1875

In response to immigration laws passed by the states, and which prove difficult to enforce, the Supreme Court decision in *Chy Lung v. Freeman* makes immigration law the responsibility of the federal government.

1880

A second wave of immigration begins arriving from southern, eastern, and central Europe. By 1920, more than 20 million immigrants arrive, most through the port of New York, and with most settling in industrializing cities of the east and Midwest.

1882

The Immigration Act of 1882 levies a tax of 50 cents per head, to be paid by shipowners, for all non-citizens arriving in US ports. The law authorizes immigration officers to screen arrivals and exclude anyone deemed a "convict, lunatic, idiot, or person unable to take care of himself or herself without becoming a public charge."

The Chinese Exclusion Act passes, barring Chinese immigrants from the United States for ten years but allowing those who were in the country as of November 17, 1880 to remain.

1891

The Immigration Act of 1891 extends restrictions to those convicted of certain crimes and to polygamists. The law also creates the first federal immigration bureau, tasked with inspecting immigrants at ports of entry and denying the sick and those barred under federal law.

Timeline

1892

Ellis Island, the United States' first immigration station, opens in New York harbor. By 1954, when the station closes, more than 12 million immigrants will pass through.

By the Geary Act, the prohibitions on Chinese immigration are extended for another ten years. All Chinese residing in the US must obtain certificates of lawful status.

1907

U.S. immigration peaks, with 1.3 million people entering the country through Ellis Island alone.

Widespread fear that Japanese workers would displace white workers in farming jobs and depress wages prompts the United States to sign the Gentlemen's Agreement with Japan. The Japanese government agrees to limit emigration to the United States to business and professional men. In return, President Roosevelt urges San Francisco to end segregation of Japanese and white students in the city's public schools.

1917

The Immigration Act of 1917 establishes a literacy requirement for immigrants entering the country. The law also establishes an "Asiatic barred zone," prohibiting immigration from British India, most of Southeast Asia, and the Middle East. Students, certain professionals, and their families are excepted. Anarchists and illiterates are also barred.

1921

By the Emergency Quota Act, immigration from each nation is limited to 3 percent of the number of foreign-born persons of that nationality already in the United States, per the 1910 census. Immigrants from the Western Hemisphere as well as temporary visitors and government officials are not subject to the quota.

1924

The Immigration Act of 1924, also known as the Johnson-Reed Act, sets more restrictive national quotas for immigration. Immigration is allowed to 2 percent of the total number of people of each nationality in the United States at the 1890 census. This quota system favors immigrants from northern and western European countries, including Great Britain, Ireland and Germany, and limits immigration from southern and eastern Europe. Immigrants from Asia are banned, with the exception of the Philippines, a US colony.

To deal with a rising tide of illegal immigrants--many of them Chinese--across the southern and northern borders, the U.S. Border Patrol is established.

1942
The United States and Mexico sign the Bracero Agreement. To deal with labor shortages caused by US entry into World War II, farm workers from Mexico are allowed to temporarily live and work in the US. US employers are required to pay for transportation and living expenses, and to pay wages equal to those of US farm workers. The program will be extended in 1949 and 1951, but end in 1964.

The Magnuson Act repeals the Chinese exclusion acts and allows Chinese nationals to become citizens.

1945
By the War Brides Act, foreign-born spouses and children of US service members are authorized entry to the United States.

1948
Europeans arriving at US ports after the end of World War II prompt Congress to pass the Displaced Persons Act, allowing the immigration of persons displaced by Nazi persecution in Europe. This is the nation's first refugee and resettlement law.

1952
The McCarran-Walter Act formally ends the exclusion of Asian immigrants to the United States and updates the national origins quota system.

Timeline

1953
The Refugee Relief Act authorizes the immigration of up to 205,000 refugees from Europe.

1956-1957
The United States admits roughly 38,000 refugees from Hungary after a failed uprising against that nation's Soviet-dominated government. During the Cold War, the United States will admit over 3 million refugees from Soviet bloc countries.

1960-1962
A secret program dubbed Operation Peter Pan admits roughly 14,000 unaccompanied children from Communist Cuba. In a further bid to help fleeing Cubans, in 1962 the Migration and Refugee Assistance Act is passed to assist refugee immigrants from the Western Hemisphere.

1965
The Immigration and Nationality Act, or the Hart-Cellar Act, ends national origin quotas dating to the 1920s. A preference system establishes seven categories of preferred immigrants, while keeping limits on immigration from specific countries and a limit on overall immigration.

1980
In the Mariel boatlift, agreed to by the US and Cuban governments, about 125,000 Cuban refugees make a dangerous sea crossing to Florida to seek political asylum.

1986
Congress passes and President Reagan signs the Immigration Reform and Control Act, also known as the Simpson-Mazzoli Act, which grants amnesty to more than 3 million immigrants living illegally in the United States.

1990
The 1990 Immigration Act allows an additional 50 percent of immigrant admissions above the level set by the IRCA of 1986.

1996

The Illegal Immigration Reform and Immigrant Responsibility Act toughens federal law on the deportation of convicted felons, expands the Border Patrol, and adds new causes for removal and for mandatory detention.

2002

The Homeland Security Act creates the Department of Homeland Security, which is given authority over the immigration system through three new agencies: Customs and Border Protection (CBP), US Immigration and Customs Enforcement (ICE), and US Citizenship and Immigration Services (USCIS).

2012

President Obama signs the Deferred Action for Childhood Arrivals (DACA), an executive order that temporarily shields undocumented immigrants brought into the United States by their parents.

2017

President Trump issues two executive orders—both titled "Protecting the Nation from Foreign Terrorist Entry into the United States"—aimed at curtailing travel and immigration from six majority Muslim countries: Chad, Iran, Libya, Syria, Yemen, and Somalia, as well as North Korea and Venezuela. Both of these travel bans are challenged in state and federal courts.

2018

Travel restrictions on Chad are lifted, while the U.S. Supreme Court upholds a third version of the ban on the remaining seven countries covered in the 2017 travel ban.

Articles

Lancaster Intelligencer and Journal (Lancaster, PA)
March 24, 1802

Immigration

The president, in his communication to Congress, never forgets the cause of the laborer, never fails to insert some expressions of tender Solicitude for his interests or of some new contrivance for his relief. Let labor be lightly burthened, take not its bread from its mouth, and many such pathetic touches, are scattered through the message and inaugural address. A stranger to this country, from reading these lamentations, would be likely to conclude that the mouth of labor was always parched with hunger, that its earnings were not secure from the unequal exactions of the government or the rapacity of individuals. If he saw the first magistrate come forward as the champion of one class of people, it would be natural to think that there was some great inequality of rights or condition which demanded this vigilant attention. But when he saw an independent yeomanry, cultivating their own estates, and rich with the fruits of their labor, he would pause for the motives of such professions and representations.

Before we rejoice in these we ought to know their sincerity, and before we yield our confidence, to ascertain their real value. To do this, let us examine some of the consequences of a particular measure and see if they do not prove these professions hollow as the wind.

One consequence of a great influx of foreigners would be a reduction in the price of labor, by increasing the number of competitors. This competition always increases in proportion to the density of the population, till the price of labor is reduced to the bare subsistence of the laborer. In Europe, and in many parts of Asia, it has long since reached the lowest mark, and when any casual or unforeseen causes have sunk it still lower thousands have died. But here the laborer settles his own price, because the demand for his labor outruns his own necessities. He feels, therefore, no abject dependence upon this or that rich man for his daily bread so long as twenty others need his services, and will pay for them at his own price. Now if we augment the number of laborers in any of our populous towns, the price will necessarily fall, from the increased competition, and if we go on with constant additions, it must in time arrive at that rate which gives nothing but the means of existence. The natural increase of our own population will eventually bring us to this point, but the vast extent of unsettled lands places it at a great distance, provided we are left to fill it up by the natural increase of our numbers.

But will the friend of the laborer offer premiums upon the importation of foreigners who will divide with you this stock of wealth and independence, and leave your children to struggle with the numerous evils of a thick population? Every influx of foreigners hastens that period which is fraught with misery and dependence. It increases the distinctions of society, by adding to the number of dependent laborers and increasing the power of the rich. The spirit of freedom evaporates in the consciousness of wants which cannot be supplied without the consent of others; servility and degradation soon become a birthright which is transmitted from father to son. The nerves and sinews of a free government are gradually weakened, till nothing short of absolute power can direct the operations of society.

Men must be influenced either by moral or physical force. If the former is diminished the latter will be increased; but somewhere there must reside a power adequate to control the actions of men, or else government must fall. Ours is a government whose operations depends in a great degree upon the existence and activity of this moral force, and as fast as this diminishes we must have recourse to a power which becomes more simple and irrefutable. Extreme dependence is the fruit of a dense population. Where then is the policy of hastening its mischiefs by any unnatural additions? Our own energies will fill the country with men with as much rapidity as provision can be made for their security and happiness. Every extraneous increase of numbers, therefore, anticipates the old age of our government. It produces wrinkles in childhood, and decrepitude in infancy, instead of advancing through the regular stages of growth and manhood.

New York Daily Herald
July 6, 1844

Immigration from Ireland

By a recent return of the numbers of Irish immigrants who have arrived during the last month in this city, and their destination, published by the agent of the "Irish Emigration Society," it appears that only a small proportion, a fifth or sixth, of these immigrants go to the country, the majority remaining in the city and its immediate neighborhood. This is very readily explained. Very few of these poor people possess the means of transporting themselves to the interior, arriving here in the most destitute condition.

We have again and again directed public attention to this matter, and suggested the adoption of some means of relieving those bands of immigrants from the deplorable destitution in which so many of them are plunged on their arrival here, and supplying them with the means of removing to the West. If the miserable demagogues who have been plundering the Irish in this country of their hard earned dollars, for the purpose of swelling the coffers of the repeal association, had a single particle of patriotism or humanity, they would have directed the enthusiastic feelings of their countrymen to some such really benevolent purpose as that we have just indicated. The money contributed in this country to the cause of repeal, and which has been employed only in filling the pockets of unprincipled scoundrels, and keeping up a mischievous agitation, would have sufficed to establish a fund for the relief and aid of Irish immigrants which would have been productive of incalculable good.

Is it ever to be in vain, to call on those who affect to be the friends of Ireland and the Irish, for some such rational and efficient manifestation of sympathy? There are many wealthy Irishmen in this city who have very properly stood aloof from the ridiculous repeal agitation; will they not come forward now and originate a movement for the extension of assistance to their poor countrymen who are landing here altogether destitute of the means of existence? Hardy, frugal, sober and industrious, these are just the class of immigrants who, in the fertile fields of the West, are certain to find comfortable homes. We do trust that something will be speedily done in this city towards the organization of an association for the relief of the Irish immigrant. A comparatively small sum would be sufficient to transport each family to the West, and purchase land adequate to its support; the sum for this purpose could be advanced in the way of a loan, to be repaid in a reasonable time. We throw out these suggestions, in this cursory manner, with the view of drawing the attention of the philanthropic to this very important subject. Let the genuine friends of Ireland and her oppressed people, if there be any such in this city, see to it that their countrymen who seek in this asylum of liberty the reward of toil and industry receive some other welcome than the yells of besotted intolerance.

Athens Post (Athens, TN)
October 4, 1850

Our Country and the Future

Under this head, we find in a monthly agricultural magazine, published in the city of Buffalo, under the title of "The Wool Grower," in the number for the last month, some observations on the condition and the destiny of our country which have even more merit than mere originality to recommend them.

The writer sets out with the general proposition that there never has been a time in our national existence when the way was so plain for the future and rapid aggrandizement of our country as at this very hour; and he demonstrates his proposition as follows:

"The overruling hand of Providence is visible in all the events of the last half century, and the finger of the Almighty points with unerring precision to what we are to expect in the coming years. The handwriting upon the wall was not more plain, while the interpretation can be made by the most simple.

"Our country now extends from ocean to ocean. From its eastern shores it has easy access to the old nations of Europe. From its western it has as easy access to the still older nations of Asia. The tide of emigration first set from the shores of Europe, and gradually peopled the Atlantic border. From the over-populous nations of Europe we have drawn largely for that population which now makes much of our power and wealth. It is safely estimated that, with the immigration from this direction, the annual increase of population is full one million—a rapid increase, but far short of what we now require to develop the immense resources of our country.

"Heretofore all the Southern portion of our country has had but little benefit directly from European immigration.

"The South requires labor, and that can only be had from a dense population. Heretofore they have had no immigrants. The door is now opened through which they can draw them to an unlimited amount. We refer to China. Already the stream begins to run this way. Even now the Chinese are flocking to our shores upon the Pacific. China is the hive ready to swarm, and she can spare us millions of intelligent, industrious, and desirable citizens, who are accustomed to labor. When they find there is a climate here as good as their own, where they can cultivate tea, and cotton, and sugar, and rear the silkworm—and the South is happily all this—they will come as rapidly as means can be furnished to bring them away. The Asiatic is destined to supplant the African, because no bar exists to a mixture of the Asiatic and European blood.

"China, then, will become to the South what Ireland has been to the North—a reservoir from whence to draw for labor, and an active population.

"It is the duty of our Government to take immediate measures to facilitate immigration from China, by causing that Government to remove all restrictions upon those subjects who wish to leave the country, and to make it an object for them to settle among us.

"Regular steam-packets should be established between Panama or San Francisco and Canton, and every possible exertion made to induce a free immigration, especially of those who understand the cultivation of tea.

"A brief statement of the climate, the advantages that they could enjoy, should be prepared and circulated through the Empire. Ample appropriations should be made by Congress, and our diplomatic relations should be placed upon the same footing as the most powerful European nations. We must not only have the trade, but we must have the surplus population of China.

"The stream of immigration from Europe has swollen to a flood. Let us have a mighty torrent from Asia. Give us an uninterrupted flow from thence for a few years, and we shall indeed become the heart and centre of the globe. And all this must transpire, as certain as the future must become the present.

"And when this does come to pass, it is easy to see the result. The South will become more densely populated than any portion of our country, and that millennium of our nation—a freedom from sectional strife for political power—will dawn upon us."

Louisville Daily Courier
June 12, 1852

The Chinese in California

One of the principal topics of public discussion throughout our State, and perhaps the only one of importance which is widely agitated at the present time, is the question of permitting Chinese labor in the mines. Since the departure of the last semi-monthly mail steamer the increase of the foreign immigration to our shores has been very great, and the class which has far outnumbered all others has been the Chinese. These people, although peaceable and honest, and in their mining operations less obtrusive than any other distinct portion of the mining community, are believed to be less advantageous to the State as citizens than any other class of laborers, on account of their parsimonious habits of life and their temporary intentions among us. Against these people in particular is the growing dislike of our miners directed, and it is the rapidly swelling tide of emigration of their countrymen that has disturbed the minds of our citizens and created doubt, apprehension, and dislike in all parts of the State.

The subject of the Chinese immigration has been transmitted to the State legislature, in an executive document, and has been discussed with some spirit, and occupied no small share of the public debate. The miners, in some sections of the gold districts, have carried the matter still further, and quite summarily and informally expelled from the diggings parties

Chinese Immigration--What Will Be Its Effect?

of Chinese who had established near them. Meetings have been held in divers places in the Northern and Southern mines, at which it has been agreed to prevent the labor of Chinese in the neighborhood represented at the meetings. No violence has yet been attempted, or is contemplated, but the diggers in some of the districts proclaim an unalterable intention not to permit Chinese labor near them.

Gov. Bigler, in his message, recommends that measures be taken by the State legislature to check this Asiatic immigration, and that aid from Congress be also invoked. He proposes for the State such an exercise of the system of taxation as shall prevent the Chinese from realizing the gains which they have hitherto enjoyed.

Here the matter rests at present. The apprehensions entertained on this subject have been exaggerated and distorted and it is, therefore, not unlikely that they will pass away as suddenly as they were created. We do not anticipate difficulty from this state of things.—*Alta Californian.*

Meigs County Telegraph
August 30, 1859

Chinese Immigration–What Will Be Its Effect?

The persistent influx of the Chinese peasantry into the United States is a fact which presses itself upon the attention alike of the political economist and the statesman. Three thousand Celestials are stated to be at this moment on their way to San Francisco. California already has a large Chinese population. Notwithstanding their characteristic vices, the Chinamen, although not popular, are found to be useful members of society. They perform, with alacrity and intelligence, the ruder kinds of labor, are marvelously frugal in their habits, and are consequently enabled to work for very low wages.

Indeed, it is not improbable that the poorer inhabitants of that vast empire, which contains within its limits nearly a moiety of the human race, may be destined to work great changes in the industrial if not in the social and political condition of America. The most obvious immediate effect of

Chinese immigration, for instance, is to supplant the negro. The Coolie in California has already made the African impossible. There, as in the West India Islands, the Malay laborer is found to be, in all respects, preferable to his darker cousin.

The voluntary immigration from Canton and Shanghai into our Pacific States bids fair soon to be enormous. Hitherto it has mainly been directed to California, but it will manifestly soon extend . . . nor is there reason to doubt that it will soon reach the Atlantic States as well.

Assuming that these natives of China may one day become as numerous among us as those of Europe, what shall their social and political status be? Are they to be regarded as whites, or people of color? Shall they, equally with emigrants from Ireland and Germany, be admitted to the benefits of our naturalization laws?—These are questions which flit and flicker now along the political horizon. But the march of events with us is rapid, and all signs conspire to prove that we have seen only the beginning of that strife of races and principles by which the institutions of the United States are, ere long, to be proved as by fire.

The National Era
March 24, 1859

Chinese Immigration and the Cause of Free Labor

To the Editor of the National Era:

The present year has brought to the philanthropists and the commercial interest alike two welcome pieces of intelligence: first, the defeat of the act laying a heavy tax on Chinese immigrants in the Upper House of the legislature of South Australia, after it had passed the Lower House by large majorities; and, secondly, the declaration by the Supreme Court of the United States of the unconstitutionality of the act of the Californian Legislature prohibiting the importation of Chinese. In both cases the "popular sentiment" of the beautiful and modest race to which you, I, and most of your readers belong, was rampant in favor of the persecuting and prohibitory laws, and it was only the "better class," or aristocratic sentiment, which upheld the rights of the colored minority.

In this connection, sir, I have to remind you that one of the obnoxious clauses of the Oregon Constitution laid a prohibitory tax upon Chinese immigrants. This point was forcibly objected to by Senator Wade last year, as making an unconstitutional and dangerous discrimination between different classes of immigrants, a discrimination which might hereafter be applied to any other unpopular class of immigrants—the English, for example. I notice this point, because I observe that in your reply to the humanitarian argument against the Oregon Constitution, you seem to have overlooked it.

Finally, I would wish to call the attention of the friends of the system of a free laboring class to the important part which the Chinese race seems destined to play in the labor system of the temperate-tropical and tropic-temperate zones of the earth's surface. While the Circassian race produces the proletaires who cultivate the cooler portions of the temperate zones, and while the African race excels in enduring labor under a tropical clime, there is an intermediate belt on both sides of the Equator, where the yellow race is, perhaps, calculated to excel both the white and black race of men. The West India islands, California, and South Australia, where the Chinese free laborer already appears and thrives, all belong to this intermediate belt. And never let us forget this important fact, that this ancient intelligent people, the children of time-worn civilization, never permit themselves to be enslaved. Wherever the Chinaman goes, there goes a free laborer. The French Emperor, in his recent letter abandoning this scheme of African immigration, as leading to Slavery, with a wise forecast of the instincts and character of this venerable people, recommends the substitution of Chinese for Congo negroes, as involving no danger of the spread of Slavery.

I had almost forgotten to notice one objection to the Chinese—that of their alleged "immorality." No impartial observer of them, as immigrant proletaires, has ever denied to them an extraordinary readiness for labor, a high appreciation of the blessings of order and good civil government, a wonderful thriftiness, and a remarkable freedom from crimes of violence and blood-shedding. Yet I think it false delicacy to conceal the handle which the Chinese give to the San Francisco "Billy Mulligans" and the ticket-of-leave diggers of Ballarat, for a Pecksniffian outcry against the "immorality" of this population. I understand that the practice of sodomy is tolerated among them. Now, I have no fear that they will succeed in infecting any European or American population with this vice, so abhorrent to the feelings of all of us; but I think there is much hope of our bringing them round to our ideas and tastes on this subject. The historical scholar, too, will not fail to remember that this practice was universally tolerated by pagan antiquity, and that a vast number of the great names of ancient Hellas and Rome are implicated with this to us odious habit; and, notably, one of the greatest of ancient moralists, Socrates, the son of Sophroniskos, who was not ashamed to confess his preference for such a connection to any the other sex could afford him.

Yet, on account of this one aberration, should we be inclined to refuse all intercourse with the virtues of Socrates, and such as he? Should we consider him unfit even to associate with the lower population of California and Australia, vicious and crime-steeped as that population notoriously is? I trow not. In the same way I affirm that the Chinese can bring into both the above-named countries many virtues, many useful qualities, not generally possessed by the laboring population of our own race. Let us not turn our backs upon them on account of their one vice, which I seek not to palliate, but which our example will probably induce them to abandon.

A salaried man myself, I already recognize in the Chinaman a political ally and comrade, soon to become powerful, and I exhort the friends of free labor to be early in the field to welcome and protect this new reinforcement to our ranks, which the progress of human intercourse has of late thrown among us. Nor less do I appeal to those generous advocates of the black and red races, not to forget that the wants of the yellow man, who is neither a savage nor a brute, but a child of civilization, call loudly for the exercise of their good offices, especially in preparing the men of our own race for the advent of this remarkable people among us. Sincerely yours, Plymouth.

The Guardian (London)
August 19, 1868

The Chinese In America

Referring to the treaty which has just been concluded between the United States and China, the New York correspondent of the Daily News says:

The treaty which Mr. Burlingame has effected overrules the last and the worst instance, in the history of the Free States, of class legislation based on a tacit denial of human equality. The laws of California relating to the Chinese are only to be compared with Carolina legislation concerning the free people of color, and they owe their origin to undisguised selfishness and fear of competition in industry, or rather in gain, since it was at the mines that the indefatigable and economical Chinese first displayed their admirable powers of acquisition.

The result has been, inevitably, that the actual treatment of the Chinese has been far worse than the legislation that discriminates against them, and which, for instance, prohibits their testifying in court against a white man, holding real estate, &c. Under this general branding of inferiority, the mean, the brutal, the unscrupulous, have cuffed and defrauded the poor Asiatics without let or hindrance, and with the full connivance of the police; while the victims, who in meekness and long suffering closely resemble the Africans, have peacefully pursued their innumerable avocations, and have overcome for the Pacific railroad the most formidable physical obstacles to its construction.

Their immigration has been as providential for the western coast as that of the Irish in days gone by for the eastern; but, except as furnishing labour when most needed for the development of a new country, there is a vast difference between these opposite accessions to the population of America.

The California statutes now abrogated by the Chinaman being put on the footing of the most favoured nationality have a shadow of excuse in the apprehension with which men regarded the introduction of so novel an element into the body politic; just as those Consular Courts in Turkey and Egypt, which Europe is now asked to abandon, were due to distrust of a people having a different religion, a different standard of morality, and a different mode of government.

Even now in the courts here a common Irishman or Irishwoman is sworn on a Bible, with a paper cross pasted on the cover, which the witness must kiss; and on one of the most frequented lines of steamboat communication with Boston, a similar Bible is kept for the steerage passengers, who are in the habit of professing utter destitution until the ordeal of the book elicits the concealed passage money.

Much more might this distrust naturally exist in the case of a pagan and superstitious race, whose object in coming to this continent was purely mercenary, and whose stay depended upon the time needed to earn the coveted affluence—even the dead being sacredly transported back to China. So exceptional a class was likely to be subjected to exceptional legislation; but the stringency of the laws, combined with the system of coolie immigration, aggravated the original evil, and kept away the better sort of Chinese, whom it is to be hoped the treaty will now tempt across, as bona fide settlers.

The number of Chinese on the Pacific coast is estimated at 50,000, of whom San Francisco has at least a third. Among these are some women, but I do not know the proportion—not enough, I fear, to keep them from being mostly prostitutes; indeed, ship loads have been imported for that purpose. Elsewhere—in Cuba, for example, among 35,000 coolies—there is not one woman for every thousand men, and the frightful immorality which this suggests is in danger of being engendered in California. Perhaps I should say was in danger. The treaty offers every inducement for the voluntary emigration of families, and the most important provision, after the equal protection of the laws, is that which admits the Chinese youth to the educational privileges of this country. This is undoubtedly the first and greatest step towards denationalisation and permanent residence, and it is only through this instrumentality that the problem of absorbing the Chinese as American citizens becomes capable of solution, like the German problem.

By this means, or our theory of government is good only for Caucasians, the Chinaman may in two or three generations take his place, and with respect, on the jury, at the bar, and in any office within the reach of talent and popularity. Until he can do that, in spite of the treaty, he will not wholly cease to be under the ban, even if he ceases to be abused and cheated, since positive outrage may now be redressed. And his progress to the condition of a full-blown American citizen promises to be one of the most interesting spectacle of the kind that the world has ever witnessed.

The progress of the American negro will be nothing to it, I mean in interest of course; for along with it we shall witness the most singular results on the side of language, with our recent annexation of Alaska will assuredly not simplify. Already in San Francisco they are publishing Japanese phrase books, and Chinese and Russian, while the streets and the mines will not soon relinquish the pigeon English and the Chinook jargon of the traders, with its Indian and Spanish elements, and which has perhaps a long lease of life yet away from the settlements.

Then in religion, we shall have what we now have, toleration of pagan idolatry in the midst of a Christian community, with perhaps the Greek church also side by side with the Catholic. Only the Mormon temple we have determined not to tolerate, because, as I conceive, of its political assumptions even more than its social.

And at all events the centre or interest has been fairly shifted from the east to the west of the Mississippi, and the completion of the Pacific railroad will make the greatest changes in the course of trade and population. The modest figure of 1,000 Chinese immigrants a month—immigrants and no longer coolies—will soon be exchanged for some significant figure per week or per day, and though the nucleus will probably always be on the Pacific coast, as that of the Irish is on the Atlantic, we may expect to meet them in all parts of our great domain, and to treat them as human if not as civilized beings.

Western Home Journal (Lawrence, KS)
September 8, 1881

The Philosophy of Migration

This year's phenomenal European immigration to this country has set the philosophers and political economists at work thinking out and explaining the cause. Their theories and opinions differ as usual upon such subjects, but some of them may hit the right reason either through chance or logic. It is true there may be a variety of causes which influence individuals to emigrate from their native country and seek new homes in a distant land and under foreign institutions. Other influences equally various may direct their steps and decide where they will build their future home, but the great mass of migration from one country to another is doubtless attributable to a common cause. It is the same general law that has ruled the migrations of nations from east to west during the whole historical period. It is as irrevocable and immutable as any of the laws of nature and is primarily the physical necessity of people to go where they can live and increase most bountifully and rapidly—where they can find most to eat, drink, and wear at least trouble and expense. This is the law of both emigration and immigration, and the application of its principles will account for the whole phenomena of European people seeking new homes in the Western world. The discovery of an outlet for Europe became a necessity, and the necessity developed the instrument just as inventions are evolved by human needs.

Sometimes it is one country, and sometimes another that furnishes the bulk of immigration to the United States. It has been Ireland; it is now Germany. The Germans have led in numbers for several years, and they seem likely to hold the advance position in the westward march for years to come. One philosopher accounts for German immigration thus:--"They know that in the United States they will not have to live in constant danger of being marched to a battlefield to enhance the glory of a sovereign, or to satisfy the ambition of a prime minister." Now, while it is true that the Germans are a peaceable people, and have been philosophized into a love of free institutions and human rights and hatred of tyranny and oppression, yet they yield the palm of patriotism to no nation on earth. When German soil is threatened by the foot of the invader, it is not the German army which repels the attack, but the German nation in arms. Even the children of the German fatherland, who have found homes in this country and exemption from military duty, have returned to Germany and then taken service for its defense in the hour of danger. They cannot be reproached with cowardly sneaking off to America for fear of war, and to avoid military service. The cause of the heavy and constantly increasing German immigration must be looked for somewhere else.

The Philosophy of Migration

The Germans are a vital and prolific people. Their vitality finds partial expression in their fruitfulness and in the matter of increase of population they can discount the French, and give the united British empire large odds in the game. They are the most prolific stock in the world, and are among the most thrifty. Their towns and cities and provinces become overcrowded by natural increase, and the laws of life lead them to find more room for their families and better opportunities for plying their trades and industries. They know better than to move from one German state, town, or section to another with the hope of improving their condition, and this country is wide and well-sprinkled with their countrymen in the enjoyment of prosperity. When they are forced to move by the conditions of their home life they follow, and that is the whole motive and spirit of emigration from any country or place, save in special cases of political or religious refugees. There is no mystery whatever in the movement, nor is there any other feature to consider in the present flood-tide of German immigration.

Most people will go to live where they can procure the necessities of life in greatest abundance and at least labor and expense, and populations multiply fastest just where there is plentiest to eat. That is the secret of the most densely populated belt of the world, and the fruitfulest zone of the earth establishes the law of migration over its surface. The discovery of the potato in this country and its transplantation and healthy growth in Ireland has made millions more Irishmen than ever could have lived without it, and rendered it possible for far more Emerald islanders to live at home than the country could otherwise have reared and supported. The history of the potato and its instrumentality in replenishing the earth has not been written, and it would be a more beneficial study for philosophers and economists than trying to discover that the present emigration from Europe is caused by anything else than the natural law of demand and supply.

Hartford Courant
May 22, 1882

Mongolian Immigration

Mr. George F. Seward has a paper on this subject in the June North American. His special qualifications for writing on it are that he spent nearly twenty years in China and that he was, during part of that time, United States minister at Peking.

Mr. Seward affirms, in flat contradiction of the Pacific coast politicians, editors and sandlot shouters, that Chinese labor, as we see it in this country, is not servile. "No slaveholding, rightly so-called, is known in China," he says. He has yet to see any proof that the Chinese laborers come here under a contract system. That some of them have borrowed money in China, agreeing to repay it out of their earnings here, is probably quite true. But as a matter of fact "the Chinese in this country are controlled by no masters; they leave service when it suits them to do so; they are almost as exacting in these respects as are the other laborers of the country.'"

Do they displace white laborers? No, says Mr. Seward. They have a practical monopoly of cigar-making in California. But no cigars "to speak of" were made in California before they came. So of shoe-making; they started the trade there. By their services in building railroads and reclaiming swamp lands they have opened new fields of profitable industry to the whites. Wages today are higher in California than anywhere else in their country, while the Chinese have reduced the cost of the necessaries of life to white laborers.

As to the alleged drain of money from this country, Mr. Seward remarks that the Chinaman lives well and dresses well when he can afford to; "he is not so far a slave to the habit of his ancestors as to wear a suit of cotton cloth and sandals of straw when he can do better, nor eat rice when a fuller diet is available." As a matter of fact, the Chinese in California dress better, he says, than other laborers, eat quite as good food, spend here (as he believes) 90 per cent of their wages, and send or take barely 10 per cent back to China. As to their "vices," of which the California moralists have had so much to say, Mr. Seward remarks that there are good men and bad among them as among us. They do not furnish an abnormal proportion of the criminals who find their way behind the bars, and "there would be fewer of them in prison if they were dealt with more liberally and justly."

"But the Chinese will not assimilate!" Mr. Seward has no patience with this line of argument. They assimilate when we let them, he says. In his twenty years' residence in China, he had opportunities for observing them, and this is his report:

I cannot recollect the moment during all these years when among the officials of the country, and among those people who had been educated more or less by contact with western people, I had not friends with whom intercourse was a matter of satisfaction and pleasure. For general kindliness, the Chinese official is not inferior to any other class of officials. For earnestness of purpose and aspiration, the Chinaman who has become a proselyte to our religion, or has observed the progressive tendencies of our civilization, leaves nothing to be desired. If they possessed less stability or character, were fickle and variable, if they would put on our garments and conform to our habits in mere externals, they would appear to the average observer in a more hopeful way; but this would not make them more worthy of esteem and confidence. If they do not assimilate, in what do they not? It is admitted that they take up with our industries. It is admitted that they are keen merchants and traders. It is admitted that they learn our language quickly. It is admitted that many join our churches. Their dress in our country is a mixture of their own and ours, they live in our kind of houses, they eat our food, they follow us in fact, about as fast and as far as we allow them to follow. I have no patience with the statement that the Chinaman is a different sort of being from ourselves. I do not agree with Senator Miller when he says that one person like Washington or Newton, Franklin, or Lincoln, has been of more service to humanity than all the Chinese who have lived and died in the lands of the Hoang-ho. Sir Frederick Bruce knew them, and said that the members of the cabinet of Peking were fit to be compared with those of any western cabinet. What was the secret of the enthusiasm of Anson Burlingame? Why has Yung Wing been sought in all American society where he has been known?

The dread of a Chinese inundation Mr. Seward regards as chimerical. He does not know of an instance in history where they have overflowed territory occupied by men of our race. They have even left intact the boundaries of their Asiatic neighbors. In thirty years less than 100,000 of them have crossed the Pacific to California. Of the women who have come a percentage have been imported for improper purposes. No doubt some criminals, paupers and diseased persons have slipped over among the healthy, honest and industrious immigrants. But Mr. Seward mildly points out that "the tendency in California has been to draw a darker picture than the facts warrant."

Three years ago, being then American minster at Peking, he proposed to the Chinese government to so supplement the provisions of the Burlingame treaty as to enable the United States to exclude undesirable Chinese immigrants of the classes above indicated, while welcoming others. That government, he says, received his proposals "in a liberal spirit." He still believes that the settlement which he undertook to effect would have been "in all respect sufficient and satisfactory." But he was overruled, and even the details of his scheme have been withheld from the public: "Called for twice by resolutions of the house and senate, the correspondence remains in the files of the state department."

It is hardly necessary, now that the mischief has been done, to follow Mr. Seward through his demonstration that the Chinese Exclusion Act of this session, besides being against public policy, is a violation of the public faith, a blotch upon our good name, and pregnant with evil consequences. We went over that ground pretty thoroughly while there was still a chance of preventing the mischief.

New York Times
October 9, 1883

The Germans In America

Among all the public anniversaries with which these latter years have been crowded for the people of this country none is more calculated to arrest attention than the second centenary of the German immigration to this continent which was celebrated yesterday. There were, indeed, many hundreds of persons of German descent or of German birth already living in this country, and especially in this state, before 1683. "New-York," says Bancroft, "was always a city of the world." But all the immigrants by way of Holland were classed together by the English of that day as Dutch, including not only Germans but French and Piedmontese. It was reserved for Penn to found upon the Delaware what he declared to be "a free colony for all mankind," and to encourage immigration by means more resembling the modern system, which is so extensive and so quietly conducted that it seems to be absolutely automatic, than had ever before his time been employed. The first organization of an emigration specifically German was his organization, and it was the result of this organization that the German-Americans of New-Jersey and Pennsylvania so heartily celebrated yesterday.

The distinction of this first German immigration to America has continued to characterize German immigration ever since. A little more than two centuries ago the map of the Atlantic coast was divided into New- France, New-England, New-Netherland, New-Sweden, and New-Spain. The Dutch settlers conquered New-Sweden, and after being themselves conquered by England and reconquered by Holland, became part of the English power, and were secured for the English side in the greater conflict which was to form the history of America for the first half of the eighteenth century, the struggle between Great Britain and France, or, as we would now say, between the Teutonic and the Latin races for the control of the New World. In all this there is no trace of German influence. There was no New-Germany, in name or in fact, among the European "claims" that were "staked out" on this continent during the seventeenth century. Indeed, there was no old mast Germany then, and the great gamesters took no account of what has since become Germany, except as spoil, in the game that they were playing for the control of two worlds.

It followed from this helplessness of the German states and their isolation from what may be called the planetary politics of the seventeenth century that the Germans who came to this country left Europe more absolutely behind them than did the immigrants of any other race. And this has continued to be their distinction ever since. The first rill of German immigration was not destined steadily to broaden and deepen into a great river. On the contrary, throughout the eighteenth century it was of little account compared with that from the islands which determined the language, the laws, and the government of this country. It was not until after the revolts of 1848 had been put down, and the insurgents began to set their faces toward the Western Republic, that the immigration from Germany became in any way comparable to that from the British islands, swelled beyond all example as this latter was in the same years by the failure of the potato crop in Ireland. Not until 1854 did the German immigration take first place in our statistics, with 206,000 immigrants against 105,000 from Ireland and 160,000 from all the British islands, in a total immigration which was not exceeded until 1872. For these last thirty years it has pretty steadily kept this first place. And it has uniformly kept its characteristic of leaving Europe behind it.

    The German immigrant, indeed, cherishes as much as any other the social ties which bind him to the land of his birth. But his renunciation of a political allegiance not merely to any potentate but to any faction in European politics is absolute and unreserved. He never asks his fellow-citizens of American birth to take sides with him in German politics. His children are taught to look to the future of America and not to the past or even to the future of Europe. There are, to be sure, a certain number of German "Reds" who try to inoculate the working men of this country with notions which never could have originated here and which have no sort of applicability to the industrial or social circumstances of this country. But the rational German-American lets these foolish persons exhaust themselves without being at all affected by them. The good citizenship of the Germans comes from the readiness with which they leave European politics behind them, and their citizenship is so good that every rational American must give them welcome and allow that the German immigration has been an unmixed good to the United States. Whatever tends to make life better worth living they have not left behind them, and would be difficult to compute the good that German immigration has done us in importing German music and German beer, and in the labors of the German immigrants as social missionaries, practically showing what was practically unknown in this country before they came, that it is possible on occasion to be idle and innocent.

Western Home Journal (Ottawa, KS)
January 9, 1886

Immigration

At the risk of being a little tedious we propose to free our mind of a little bile on the question of immigration. We start upon the hypothesis that it is the one important practical question of interest to the people of Kansas. The national issues which have excited the people of this State more than any other, and which have found here their firmest defense and fullest illustration, may be regarded as so far settled as to allow us to pay a little attention to the things that make for our material peace. We will risk the State on the vital issues. She will be as true to them as the needle to the pole. We will risk her also to discriminate between what is vital and what is venal, between what is true and what is false, between what is progress and what is retrogression. The status of the State is at last tolerably well fixed. Radical for the right, she is conservative of it after it is secured. Progressive in everything that promises the welfare of society, she is not ready to rush into every experiment which false progressives would inaugurate. We can now count upon her future action with a tolerable degree of comfort. We put her down any time for genuine Republicanism, but no time for all the nonsense which some Republicans may choose to christen by the name.

But there are other questions which come home to our interests, and appeal to all that is near to us in our personal welfare. Everything which tends to the development of the industrial resources of the State has a bearing upon our persons and our purses which, it would naturally be supposed, would require no argument to interest us in. And yet, while everybody acquiesces in this general statement, very few seem to be awake to the particular fact upon which it bears. We have from time to time called the attention of our readers and of the proper authorities to the magnitude of this subject; we have shown by figures that a fearful disproportion of the immigration into the West is against us, especially of that portion of it which can be influenced by immigration agencies; we have contrasted the activity and the enterprise of other Western States with the lethargy and inefficiency of our own; we long ago called the personal attention of the authorities who ought to be awake to the subject to its importance, and freely volunteered any advice or assistance which we could give in the premises, and we have become so far disgusted with our efforts that we do not propose to repeat them in the same direction. But we are in no notion of relinquishing the agitation. We shall make our appeal to the people—to those who have the taxes to pay and need company to divide the amount and lessen the burden. It will be their own fault if this miserable state of respectable imbecility and costly inefficiency continues.

The one question which, next to sound Republican principle, ought to be paramount to every other in the next State election, is the question of immigration. To cover these vast unoccupied prairies with intelligent settlers, to lessen our taxes by increasing our taxpayers, to fill the places of lazy aborigines with enterprising Anglo-Saxons, in short, to fill this splendid State with a population commensurate with its era and worthy of its capabilities should be the business of the State Department for the next two years. Men should be chosen to office qualified for this work and personally interested in its prosecution. It is for this reason alone that we mentioned the name of Mr. Walker last week in connection with the governership. We have no axe for him to grind—not even a hatchet. We have no personal interests to subserve in his election. But he is an extensive landowner, is thoroughly acquainted with immigration movements, and would be personally interested in a vigorous, organized, and effective effort to induce immigration into Kansas. This is why we would like to see him governor. Those who think it more important to have the offices farmed out fairly, and that the chief end and aim of the State Department is to attend to the distribution of pap and to the chances for the succession, will not be particularly impressed with either our views or our men. It is not with such that we argue. We are aware that there are those who say that nothing more can be done than is being done, and that immigration is coming in as fast as could be expected. We know it is coming, but we know also that it is coming not on account of effort, but in spite of it. It is coming, not because we help it, but because it cannot help coming. Nine-tenths of the immigration westward ought to come here. The attractions of no other state begin to compare with ours. And that vastly more can be done than has been done must be evident to anybody. The success which has attended local effort shows what can be done on a broader scale.

The town of Ottawa has a population of two thousand, with a corresponding number settled and settling in the country around. This is the result of three years' vigorous and systematic effort to induce persons to come here. It is the result of liberal and judicious advertising; of an innumerable number of private letters; of public speeches and addresses; of just such effort as, conducted on a broader basis and aiming at wider results, would give Kansas from half a million to a million inhabitants during the next gubernatorial term. Our town has not been built by railroad excitement, for we have had none, and until very recently, were very dubious about getting one. Our location was good, but no better than many others. There is just as good an opportunity to make a town twenty-five miles west of here as there was here. The result is solely due to energetic and well-directed effort. We speak of it, not by way of boast, but by way of illustration. What has been done here can be done on a larger scale, if the people will put the offices into the hands of men capable of doing it. And we say once for all, that we neither ask nor could accept the service, however desirable it might be, if it were tendered us; and our only reason for saying this is to prevent the impression that our views are inspired by any sinister ambition. Under the present circumstances, we know of nothing so important to us personally, or to the people generally, as a big immigration into the state. Our candidate for governor, other things being equal is the man who can bring it.

Weekly Commonwealth (Topeka, KS)
January 14, 1886

Labor Bureau Report

Some days ago we published extracts from the report of Mr. Button, commissioner of the Labor Bureau, and now continue those extracts. The paragraphs are from letters received in answer to circulars sent out:

Foreign Labor—Immigration.

I know that foreign immigration is injurious to the American workingman, especially to my business, and I think that some legal restriction should be placed upon it.—Railroad brakeman.

I think foreign immigration is the cause of the present hard times. I am not opposed to a man because he is a foreigner, but I think there are too many here for the work there is to do. I think our government should stop immigration, or else provide more work for its native citizens.—Teamster.

I am in favor of stopping all immigration of foreign labor, and killing all Chinamen and negroes.—Teamster.

I do not know that recent immigration has affected the business of teaching, but I am opposed to the unlimited immigration of inferior races.—Teacher.

I do not think that foreign immigration has had any effect on my trade.—Painter.

I believe that the importation of foreign labor under contract is an unmitigated evil, and designed, if not stopped, to undermine the foundations of our government.—Stone Cutter.

Immigration of foreign labor is a curse. I am a skilled mechanic, and have been out of work two-thirds of the time for the last year, because I could not get work to do; and I have a family to support. Nero fiddled when Rome was burning, and that is just what, in my judgment, the "better classes" (what a misnomer, in this land of equality!) of this republic are doing today.—Mason.

I think foreign immigration is injurious to American labor, and that it should be stopped, if labor expects to prosper.—Street Car Driver.

My business has not been as good this year as in previous years; less work, and the pay harder to get. I think the cause is too much foreign immigration, and that it should be controlled in some way, or American labor will be reduced to a level with foreign paupers.—Shoemaker.

I don't say the depression in business and the low rates of wages to recent immigration, but rather to the damnable avariciousness of wealth, and the creed it holds, that a worker—male or female—has no right to live save in slavery. My opinion is, that to improve labor, it is necessary to elect wage workers to the state legislature and to congress, that we may get laws passed that will benefit the workingman. Of course this is from a foreign born citizen, but the records will prove that I served three years to put down rebellion to a republican government, and to strike the shackles from 4,000,000 of slaves. I hope the day will never come for another war in this county, but it seems to me that the white wage workers today in this great free republic are in many respect not as well off as was the black man in the south prior to 1861.—Shoemaker.

The immigration of foreign labor has no effect upon the printer's trade.—Printer.

Foreign immigration does not affect my trade as it does others.—Printer.

I have been in the state seven years and my trade has been rapidly growing worse. I think the influx of people from other states and countries is an evil. The cost of food, clothes and rent remain the same, while wages are decreasing.—Plasterer.

Foreign labor is injurious to all mechanics, more or less. There are more workmen than work; one can see that by visiting any city.—Stone Mason.

I have been in Kansas twenty-one years, and I find times growing worse, surplus labor seems to be the cause.—Bricklayer.

I think Chinese labor detrimental and demoralizing, and want them sent out of the country and kept out.—Painter

The stoppage of foreign immigration would be a benefit to my trade, which is not so good this year as formerly. There is less to do and more to do it.—Paper Hanger.

Foreign immigration has had no effect on my trade.—Paper Maker.

My wages have been reduced 25 cents per day for the past four years, by reason of foreign contract labor.—Paper Maker

The immigration of foreign laborers under the contract system does not affect us here, but free foreign laborers do. They have a bad effect on our trade, they work for less wages, and are willing to take old clothes and other truck for pay. We need protection against the foreigners themselves worse than we do on the product of their labor while they stay at home.—Carpenter.

Stop foreign immigration.—Deputy Marshal.

Foreigners coming to this country are willing to accept much lower wages than are native workmen, and employers hire them without regard to who or what they are, consequently American workmen must work for less than they should, on account of this unjust competition. I am in favor of radical action in this matter. The great outcry against the Chinaman is ridiculous, when we consider that other foreigners work about as cheap as they do. Stop them all, if any.—Stone Mason.

Anything that will absorb the surplus labor and prevent an increase will be beneficial. Unlimited foreign immigration is injurious to the interests of labor, in my estimation.—Stone Mason.

There are none more hurtful to our trade than the imported Italians or Swedes. As a rule, they know little about mason work. They are employed at reduced prices, which enables them to procure more steady employment from contractors taking government work. There should be a law forbidding the employment of contract foreign labor on all government work.—Stone Mason.

I am opposed to Chinese labor.—Machinist.

Foreign contract labor has a bad effect on all workingmen and should be prohibited, and the Chinese must go.—Machinist.

In regard to Chinese labor, I for one wish them expelled from the country, as they are a great scourge and plague.—Machinist.

Immigration of foreign laborers has had no direct effect on my trade, but I think it is detrimental to the wage workers of the country generally.—Machinist.

Have not been in the battle of life long enough to take observation, and therefore have no remarks to make. The immigration of foreigners has not, to my knowledge, affected my trade.—Machinist apprentice.

Foreign immigration has had a bad effect, and should be restricted.—Machinist.

No effect that I have noticed.—I a laborer.

Foreign imigration has had a very bad effect, and I think it should be stopped if our government considers the welfare of American labor. I believe proper legislation would very much improve the condition of the working people if it could be had.—Engine Wiper.

Both free and contract immigration have had a decidedly bad effect on my trade.—Railroad Laborer.

Foreign immigration is an injury to all laboring people in this country.—Packing House Laborer.

I think the more foreigners that come here, the harder it is for American citizens to get a living.—Laborer.

Combination of all wage-workers for the purpose of influencing legislation to stop all kinds of foreign immigration.—Laborer.

There is a gang of Italians here, working on a job of river improvement for the United States government. These men were brought here under contract, and are farmed out by a padroon, who receives their pay; they work cheaper than Americans, and cannot speak English; they spend very little, have no families and no homes.—Laborer.

I believe foreign immigration keeps down wages.—Laborer.

It is a detriment to the country, and should be stopped.—Laborer.

No effect on my labor.—Packing House Laborer.

I believe that too much immigration is the principal cause of the hard times.—Laborer.

I think the present hard times are caused by the rapid improvements in labor-saving machinery, coupled with the large number of foreign laborers brought into our country.—Shoemaker.

Foreign immigration gluts the labor market, and fills the country with "tramps." No laborer with a family can get twenty days' supplies ahead. Labor needs and should demand relief at the hands of congress. It should insist upon a redaction of rents on town and farm property, and a lower rate of interest.—Laborer.

Foreign immigration has filled the country with a large amount of surplus labor, and I see no remedy unless we have another war, so as to have a lot of us killed off and make room for the balance.—Carpenter.

Can't say as to my trade.—Laborer.

Bad for harness makers.—Harness Maker.

I don't think that immigration has much effect on railroaders.—Locomotive Fireman.

My opinion is that judicious legislation and the prevention of foreign immigration would improve the condition of laboring people in this country.—Expressman.

It has not affected me directly, but I think it should be stopped.—Stationary Engineer.

I can't say that foreign immigration has had any effect on my business; don't think it has. I think our hours are rather long, considering the wages paid. We are called up at all hours of the night, and have to work part, at least, of every Sunday.—Druggist.

Immigration has worked a great injury to my trade, as foreigners are largely wood workers.—Cabinet Maker.

When the cup is full, if you try to put in more it will overflow. Five hundred foreign paupers will displace that many citizens. Corporations, in trying to beat each other, employ cheap labor, and pauperize American labor, thereby destroying the prosperity of the country, and effectually ruining themselves.—Carpenter.

Foreign labor does not hurt me much. I find no trouble in getting work. Have not been out of a job for sixteen years more than three days.—Railroad Machinist.

Honorable immigration does not hurt my trade, but contract foreign labor brought to this country by corporations is a burning disgrace on American civilization; it is a new thing in American history.—Railroad Carpenter.

Foreign immigration should be stopped, or greatly restricted, if the standard of American citizenship is to be kept up. I believe that legislation should be in the interests of labor, instead of in the interest of gambling and speculation.—Carpenter.

I am opposed to promiscuous immigration, and in favor of a lower tariff.—Carpenter.

Not directly on my trade, but it should be stopped.—Railroad Carpenter.

I object to the importation of Chinamen and all other foreigners under the contract system, as it is virtually making slaves of them, and is dangerous to our own institutions.—Carpenter.

In my opinion, foreign immigration cuts no figure in the wages of the American worker. This country is capable of supporting ten times its present population. The more workers, the more consumers. The great curse to labor can be summed in one word, and that word is, monopoly—land monopoly, money monopoly, transportation monopoly. I would suggest that to permanently improve the condition of labor, the government issue all money direct to the people; own and control all telegraph lines and lines of transportation. No person allowed to hold more land than he or she can occupy and cultivate. Repeal the protective tariff. Adopt the eight hour law for every trade and calling. Then, with free trade, free land, free money, and free immigration, we would get the best people of the old world to help develop the resources of the new. We would become the great manufacturing and commercial nation of the earth; in fact, we would be supreme in everything that goes to make a great and powerful nation.—Laborer.

The importation of foreign labor has almost destroyed the trade. In all factories the work is being done by cheap workmen from some of the German states, and my observations are that they are not so skillful or swift as our native workmen, and are more inclined to slight their work. It is but natural for men with money to buy muscle much as they would buy wheat, or corn or any other commodity, always in the cheapest market—and Europe is the cheapest. Place a protective tariff on imported labor, and capital will absorb your own labor. For more than twenty years you have fostered the manufacturing of skilled goods; why not foster the skill that makes them?—Cabinet Maker.

Immigrants brought from England by my employer have caused a decided reduction in wages. Twice a year he brings men to this country, who for a while work cheaper than the average citizen; besides, he advertises in eastern and southern papers, which brings a large surplus of labor to this city, and if we ask for more pay we are told that there are lots of men anxious for our jobs. Most of our force at this writing are not averaging four days' work a week, so you see the policy of enticing a lot of surplus labor here to keep men at starvation wages. This concern is English. None of them are naturalized, and they don't care a cent for American institutions. There is no change in the price of living, although the packing houses buy beef for less than two cents per pound on foot and sell for ten to twelve and a half cents, and hogs and sheep in proportion. The average workingman can't afford meat oftener than once a day for himself and family. Tenement houses with four and five families and poor ventilation are unhealthy; but one family should be allowed in a house. Give us steady employment, decent homes and fair wages, and there would be no cause for complaint.—Butcher.

Numerous foreigners entering factories as apprentices, for a mere pittance, have nearly driven Americans out of my trade.—Broom Maker.

The apprentice system has done as much to reduce wages in the broom business as any other cause. Nearly all apprentices are foreigners, and are secured for a mere pittance. Thus in a short time they have deprived old experienced workmen of work, or have so reduced their wages that they are now below living figures.—Broom Maker.

Foreigners are indenturing their children as apprentices for sums that amount to nothing, and our trade is about ruined.—Broom Maker.

Foreign labor has not directly affected my trade, but indirectly it has done so, as it has a tendency to lessen wages in all branches of labor by creating a surplus. The letting of our public work by contract has a disastrous effect upon wage-workers, because bidders underbid until they have to crowd down wages, or swindle the state. My business has been poorer this year than for four years previous. I was a soldier of the rebellion, and receive a pension. I believe the government should own and control all railroads and telegraph lines for the benefit of the state.—Brick-layer.

I think the laboring classes, as a whole, get a meager support; they get barely enough to live from day to day; if they lose any time, they must of necessity go in debt. In regard to foreign immigration, I think it has greatly injured the laboring class; it has reduced the wages of all mechanics. Laws of supply and demand govern the price of labor to a greater or less extent, and when we come in contact with these foreign mechanics, we find them bidding down very low.—Bricklayer.

In the first place I consider that under the present state of government and society, the whole system by which affairs are carried on among us, that the immigration of foreign labor, under contract or otherwise, is certainly a detriment to all labor. Now my judgment in regard to improving our condition is this: A general reorganization of the government, and the establishment of a socialistic form, which in my opinion is the only scientific and just method. Now in order to bring this about in a peaceable manner, which I hope will be done, it is necessary to have all working classes, and as many of the other classes as wish, to assist us in this matter, unite with us in our organizations, and become educated in this movement. Set the workingman to thinking. Get him to understand that he and every person who creates wealth has a right to it—all of it—not the mere pittance he receives, which barely keeps himself and family from starving. It is my honest belief that this is the only way we can ever better our condition. So let us work for its peaceful revolution.—Carpenter.

Co-Operation

It seems to me that workingmen should, and could, become their own employers. They not only create the capital, but supply it for all improvements and industries. The system of building railroads, as practiced in this country, could be managed as well by the men who do the work as those who only furnish the credit. All that is required is for them to study this matter and become familiar with it, and they will find it easy to become their own employers. The banking business should be conducted by the working people, thus becoming their own depositors as well as the custodians of their own money, instead of committing it to the tender mercies of embezzlers and note shavers.

More independence. Seek to run our own trade, as it was thirty years ago. Loiter around no place begging for work. Start co-operative shops. Our fathers started out with the assertion that "all men were created equal." Let us try and prove that they did not lie.—Carpenter.

San Francisco Examiner
November 11, 1891

The Slaughter Continues

Suey Sing Tongs Even Up the Score

With the Suey On Tongs

An Industrious Harnessmaker Is The Latest Victim

He Is Ambushed by the Hatchet Men and Shot to Death From Behind to Avenge the Wounding of Young Yek Hi, the Last Suey Sing Tong Man Hurt in the Feud—No Witnesses to Be Found

The Suey Sing Tong highbinders have again squared accounts with the Suey On Tong.

Chin Sing Suck, a member of the last-named society, was found dead in Spofford alley yesterday morning with two bullet holes in him.

While no one can be found who saw the shooting, the evidence is conclusive that the highbinders of the Suey Sing Tong killed him in order to avenge the shooting of Young Yek Hi, who was shot in the neck by the hatchet men of the Suey On Tong.

The account of dead and wounded of each society now balance, and the Chief of Police thinks the feud will stop for a time at least.

As far as can be ascertained, the last dead man had not done anything particular to deserve or provoke killing. He was not a highbinder, but a peaceable, industrious Chinaman. He was, however, handy to get at, and, as the Suey Sing Tongs needed a man to even up the score, they took him.

The first tidings of the killing reached the Police Station at 6:45 in the morning.

A citizen who had happened to pass by Spofford alley came to the police station and reported that a Chinaman was dying.

Captain Douglass sent Policemen Webster and Amos Williams to investigate. They soon telephoned in that the Chinaman was dead. The Morgue wagon was sent for the body.

Two Bullets In His Body

When Webster and Williams turned into Spofford alley, which is a narrow passageway from Clay to Washington street, above Dupont, they found the little street thronged with excited Chinese. In the middle of the block, in a depression formed by the wearing out of the plank pavement, lay the body of a well-dressed Chinaman. There was a pool of blood about him. He lay on his face. One ball had gone through his body and the other had passed in his neck, through the mouth and out of his upper lip, knocking out the upper front teeth.

The police learned that he had fallen on his back, but that some of the Chinese had rolled him over. Both bullets ranged upwards, showing that the shooter—or shooters, for there may have been two or more in the ambush—were below him when the killing was done.

On the east side of the alley are several cellar ways, just the places for a man to lay in wait. On the west side there is a doorway that would answer almost equally well.

Chin Sing Suck lived a few doors nearer Washington street than these places. He had slept there the night before and was undoubtedly on his way to work when he was assassinated.

The hatchet men doubtless knew his habits and knew that 6:30 o'clock in the morning was a good time to catch him, for the night police squad leave Chinatown at 6 o'clock and the day men do not come on until some time later. This, of course, made their chance of escaping very good.

The Slaughter Continues

On the east side of the street is a Chinese cook shop. It is down in one of the cellar-ways already referred to.

Shot From A Cellarway

When Detectives Cox and Glennon, whose specialty is Chinatown crime, started in their hunt for the slayer or slayers of Chin Sing Suck they found a bullet-hole through a Chinese sign above the cellar cook shop. The bullet-hole was only a foot or so above the sidewalk. Its path through the inch board was nearly level. They went on up the alley, following the course of the bullet, and soon found it imbedded in an upraise on the sidewalk. The course of the bullet showed that the weapon from which it was fired was held at the same level—eight inches or a foot above the sidewalk—and a dozen feet or so back from the perforated sign is another cellarway. There is where the murderer probably hid.

On the brick wall on the same side of the street is the mark of another bullet.

People near there heard four shots, and the bullet marks would seem to indicate that the manner of the murder was this:

Chin Sing Suck left his room in the Ng Young Company's quarters, 59 Spofford alley, as usual at about 6 o'clock and crossed to the cook shop to get his breakfast. One of the avengers of the last Suey Sing Tong man shot posted himself in a cellarway to wait for the victim to come out. From his post he would have a fair chance at the man's back as he ascended the stairs from the cook-shop door.

More Than One Assassin

He took his chance as Chin Sing Suck came upstairs, and missed. This would account for the shot that went through the signboard and buried itself in the sidewalk. Chin Sing Suck, who must by this tune have nearly gained the street, naturally made a run for safety. His room only a few doors below was the most likely place for him to make for, and he started for it. Then another assassin took a shot from his position in the doorway opposite. He also missed, and his bullet it was that dented the brick wall. The victim would naturally spring aside as he saw the flash from the doorway, and that would bring him close to the other highbinder.

Reporting: Immigrants 1803-1931

The latter from his place on the cellar steps had an excellent chance, as the man ran by, and evidently he improved his opportunity. Two shots went into Chin Sing Suck from the right side, both ranging up. The highbinder's low position on the steps would explain the course of the bullets.

Chin Sing Suck fell then in the hollow in the street and died there, and his slayers, their duty to their clan well done, made their escape.

The body was not robbed. In the dead man's pockets was found a bankbook showing a deposit of $813.82 in the San Francisco Savings Union. There was also a silver watch and chain and $5.80 in coin.

The dead Chinaman was a horsecollar maker employed in Ewing Bros.' harness factory. Ha had worked there for six years.

Several Witnesses, But None Will Talk

The detectives learned there were several witnesses to the murder, for the alley at that time in the morning is always frequented by Chinese on their way to work.

But though they questioned many of the Chinese who must have been in the vicinity, they could not gain an admission from one of them that he saw the shooting. They know that the hatchet men are as ready to kill a man who gives evidence against them as they are to murder in the regular course of business, and believe with reason that the man who told on the highbinders would not be allowed to live This fact makes things very hard for the Chinatown detectives, and unless some Chinaman in sympathy with the Suey On Tong men saw the shooting the murderers are not likely to be found. However, the dead man's society, which would as soon use the foreign devil's law as a pistol or a knife to get even, may be depended on to do all it can to find the killers.

An autopsy was made on the dead man at the Morgue, and it was found that the bullet that went in at the neck had cut the jugular vein. The other entering on the right side of the back went through the stomach and kidneys. Either was enough to cause death.

Police Station in Chinatown

"There is no place of meeting for the highbinders now," said Chief Crowley yesterday, "as we have broken their headquarters up. They simply pass the word along when a shooting has to be done. They will not swear against one another, nor give the police a single bit of information. If they did what would be their reward? Why, if a Chinese testified here in the courts in a highbinder case he would be shot on his return to Chinatown. In a personal fight the police can get all the information wanted, but where the highbinder societies are involved nobody sees anything. Highbinders themselves are sworn to secrecy and outsiders among the Chinese have a dread of meddling in their fights—they don't want to be shot.

"We have to keep extra men in Chinatown. Still these fellows defeat us. A year ago I wanted to have a station built right in the heart of the Chinese quarter, but my suggestion was laid aside. Today Major Hammond, through the Board of Police Commissioners, has addressed a communication to the Board of Supervisors asking them to establish a police station in Chinatown. Of course, this station would be an expense to the city, but it is absolutely necessary to keep these Chinese quiet. It might have a good effect on them, for they have never done any shooting while the police were around.

"Chinatown is thinning out rapidly and many merchants have been forced to close up their stores and go back to China, and, though there are a great number of Chinese in town now, they will be scattered before next summer to the interior, Mexico and China. They will have no means of making a living here.

"Lyman Mowry told me a few days ago that, in his opinion, there will hardly be a Chinese in Chinatown five years from now."

San Francisco Examiner
March 13, 1893

Crime Among The Chinese

Highbinders Who Murder and Rob and Escape Arrest

Chief Crowley On The Subject

The Head of the Police Department Discusses the Recent Shootings and Methods for the Suppression of the Murderous Tong Men--Straw Bond Facilities and the Methods of Police Court Clerks.

The present highbinder war was inaugurated on February 20th, when six members of the Bo Sin Sear Tong raided the store of Lee Sun, a Bing On Tong man. They wrecked the store and fired a number of shots, one of which hit An Law, a laborer, in the leg, and another penetrated the back of Chin Doo Poo, a musician.

Then some Suey On Tong men one night raided a house belonging to Bing On Tong men. They demanded money and tore earrings, bracelets and rings from the women inmates.

The next outbreak occurred between members of the Suey On and Bing On Tongs on the corner of Jackson and Stockton streets. Many shots were exchanged, but the only disaster occurred to Ching Ho, a Chinese woman who was passing. She was shot in the right arm and right leg. Her wounds were not dangerous.

The Chinese Six Companies interfered at this point and offered a reward of $200 for the arrest of the highbinders. Then by general consent hostilities were suspended until after the New Year festivities.

The war was renewed on Monday afternoon, March 6th, at 2:30 o'clock, when Ah Kee, a laborer, was shot by Wong Fun, a Hop Sing Tong member. Ah Kee died of his injuries after having identified Wong Fun.

On Tuesday, March 8, Chung Que, a Hop Sing Tong man, was fatally shot by Ham Wong, a member of the Suey Sing Tong. The shooting occurred in Sullivan alley, and the murderer was arrested shortly after the occurrence.

Crime Among the Chinese

On Friday, March 10, Quong Hing and Wong Jack, Hop Sing Tong men, assisted by a number of others, led an attack on a party of Suey Sing Tong men in Washington alley, near Jackson street. About fifteen shots were exchanged, one of the highbinders receiving a flesh wound in the neck. He was concealed by his companions.

Standing on chair or stool in the office of Chief of Police Crowley at the Old City Hall, one may look out the window and take in at a glance almost the entire scene of the highbinder war now going on in the Chinese quarter. From this window it is almost possible to see the spot where, only few weeks ago, a Chinese druggist who had refused to obey the insolent commands of one of the clannish tongs was sprawled face downward on the pavement with a bullet from a highbinder's pistol through his body.

One can walk up Washington street from the Old City Hall one block and a half, turn into Waverly place and be confronted by the big star-bedecked lanterns in front of a police station in the very heart and center of Chinatown.

Walk along the streets of the Chinese quarter now at any hour of the day or night and at short intervals you will meet policemen patrolling the streets. They travel in pairs. Policemen always do that in the Chinese quarter here.

What The Highbinders Do

One would think it impossible that groups of rival highbinders could gather on the open streets in broad daylight and, at places where a policeman may be soon almost constantly and where the popping of their pistols can almost be heard by the head of the Police Department, draw their revolvers, exchange from ten to thirty shots, kill or wound either one of the factions or an innocent passer-by, dart into some of the numerous holes in the wall leading to none but themselves know where and make their escape right from under the very eyes of the police.

But such events have been of frequent occurrence in this city; so frequent, in fact, as to cause editorial comment in one of the leading journals of New York City, where they have a Chinatown in miniature and where the trickery and cunning of the Mongolian lawbreakers have caused the police proportionately as much annoyance as here.

Reporting: Immigrants 1803-1931

The question of crime in Chinatown and the police methods of dealing with the highbinders, made the subject of editorial comment by the New York Press, was brought to the attention of Chief of Police Crowley yesterday, and after he had read the editorial reflecting so harshly on the lack of efficiency in his department he was asked:

"Why is it that the same criminal conditions do not exist in the Chinese quarters in New York and other Eastern cities as here?"

Here and in the East

"There are various reasons," replied the head of the San Francisco police department. "In the first place there are more Chinese in one block in this city than can be found in the entire Chinese quarter of Now York. I will say that in one block on Dupont street, between Jackson and Clay streets, there are at this moment more Chinese than in all New York. There are between 12,000 and 14,000 Chinese in this city now according to estimates made yesterday by the Chinese consul and myself. Perhaps there are more. Some of my men who are thoroughly familiar with Chinatown believe that there are 20,000 of them here. Now that is one good reason. It is much easier to handle and watch 3,000 men than it is to do the same for 15,000, and there are not 3,000 Chinese all told in the city of New York. I do not believe that there are 2,000, while in Chicago there are not more than 200.

"Now in New York city inspector of police Byrnes has at his command 4,000 men. Of this number he can place 2,000 on the street at any time, or enough men, if necessary, to have one policeman for each Chinaman in that city. Here it is different. I have all told 450 men. This includes captains, sergeants, corporals, men assigned to office and special duties, patrolmen and all. With this number I am compelled to so arrange them as to give police protection to an area larger than that of the city of New York. I cannot send my entire force into Chinatown. The detail there consists of the Chinatown squad of five policemen, in addition to the usual patrol. This, of course, makes up the force when the rival gangs of highbinders are at peace. When trouble breaks out, such as we have had to contend with during the past few weeks, the force is at once increased, and now I have twenty or more men there, and it's a shame, too, that I am compelled to keep such a number of men there.

Crime Among the Chinese

Thinks The Force Efficient

"I consider my men as efficient as the police of New York. I believe that we have a better class of men on the police force in this city than in any other place on earth, and I can tell you that if the same conditions existed in New York as exist here there would be as much crime proportionately in the Chinese quarter of that city as here, and Inspector Byrnes would have as much trouble in combating it as I have."

"What conditions do you mean?"

"Do you think for a moment," said Chief Crowley, "that anybody can obtain release on worthless bonds as easily in New York or any other place as in this city? No, sir. The 'straw bond' practice carried on here has more effect in defeating the efforts of the police in checking crime in Chinatown than can be overcome. The other day there was a conference between the police judges and myself on the question of bonds in Chinese cases, and it was agreed that bonds should not be accepted unless they were known to be good. The Chinese consul, whom I consider a firm, courageous and honest man, and who is doing all he can to help me in this matter, agreed to have all the bonds offered looked into and pass upon their genuineness before they were accepted and the prisoner released. That day my men brought in about thirty Chinese they knew, as well as anyone can know without positive evidence to be highbinders. They charged them with vagrancy and locked them up. It had, as I said before, been agreed that those men should not be released on bonds unless it was shown that the sureties offered were good.

Work of Police Court Clerks

"Then what happened? Why, two police court clerks, in defiance of the wishes of their superiors, accepted whatever bonds were offered and those highbinders were released to at once make their way back to Chinatown to shoot and kill. These bonds, I suppose, are all worthless.

"There are a stack of bonds a foot high in the hands of the attorneys employed by the city to collect forfeited bonds. They are not worth the paper they are written on. I have thirty or more Chinese in jail now. They are highbinders charged with vagrancy. I suppose they will be set at liberty on bonds accepted by police court clerks, who are always in convenient call when the outside friends of a prisoner seek to secure his release.

"You don't suppose that these police court clerks take these bonds for nothing, do you? I don't. It is a source of revenue, and I propose going before the Board of Supervisors and see if something cannot be done to stop this wholesale acceptance of bonds by the clerks. They should not be allowed to take a bond in a Chinese case, or for that matter in any case. It is a corrupt system, and more than anything else is responsible for the prevalence of crime in the Chinese quarter. Do you suppose that such a condition exists in New York? There the court officials aid the police. Here it looks as if the clerks of police courts for the sake of pecuniary gain side with the criminals. My men arrest a well-known highbinder and charge him with vagrancy. He is scarcely locked up when his friends make out a bond in which fictitious addresses and values are given. They swear to it, a police court clerk accepts it and the prisoner is allowed to go. When his case is called, of course he fails to appear and the bond is forfeited. When an effort is made to collect the bond no such men as are named as the sureties can be found."

Difficulties of the Police

"Why is it that so few arrests for murder are made among the Chinese?"

"We have six men downstairs now charged with murder, despite the fact that unless a policeman happens to be right on the scene of shooting detection is almost impossible. They are the hardest people in the world to obtain information from, and any one familiar with the Chinese quarter, with its many side streets and alleys, its narrow, underground passageways and the thousand and one nooks and corners, can at once appreciate the difficulties the police have to contend with.

"It is almost impossible to get one Chinaman to testify against another. They won't do it. Then the fact that we do not understand their language is a great obstacle in the matter of the detection of criminals. You will notice that when a shooting takes place in Chinatown the place selected is never in one of the flush blocks—that is, a block not cut up by one or more alleys. The highbinders always do their shooting near one of those convenient avenues of escape, and if a policeman is not on the spot the as-

Crime Among the Chinese

sassins dart into these narrow passageways which are always crowded, up a stairway or down into some hole in the ground, and by the time a policeman reaches the spot what does he find? Nothing but a crowd of jabbering Chinamen, whose only answer to all questions is 'No sabe.'

"I believe that all the men under me work hard to check crime in the Chinese quarter. During the past twelve years this department has made over 16,000 arrests in that quarter of the city alone, and in that same period over $300,000 in fines has been collected. I think that this is a good showing."

"What effect did the establishing of the Waverly Place Police Station have?"

"A good effect for a long time after it was opened, but with the men at my disposal I am unable to keep a reserve force there."

What the Chief Suggests

"How would you break up the present trouble in Chinatown? What means do you think would prove effective in suppressing the highbinders?

"If I had men enough to keep three or four policemen constantly on every block in Chinatown these shooting affrays would, I believe, soon cease. Then it would be possible to have a policeman on hand at the first report of a pistol. The highbinders would stand then comparatively little show of escaping. When the first shooting in the present outbreak occurred some weeks ago I ordered a special detail into Chinatown. While the men were kept there no shooting occurred. The day the special detail was removed, when everything was thought to be quiet, there was more shooting. But I can't keep three policemen on duty on every block in Chinatown. The men cannot be spared from other parts of the city, and the only way of suppressing the highbinder is to keep him constantly under the eye of a policeman, that and the doing away with the straw bond practice now indulged in by the clerks of the police courts.

Assistance from the Chinese

"The Chinese consul is doing all that he can to assist me. He has gone as far as to notify those merchants who are now compelled to pay tribute to the highbinder organizations that they must cease doing so at once. If they do not they will themselves be placed under the ban as highbinders. This is having a good effect, and the merchants are forming what might be termed a vigilance committee. I am in hopes that much good will result from this organization of Chinese merchants. If we can ever fix it so that one Chinese will go into court and testify against another, or give information that will help us in the identification of Chinese charged with or suspected of crime, then we will be able to work against this class of criminals more successfully. But all this has been promised us before," said the Chief, "and I can't say that much ever came of it."

San Francisco Call
August 4, 1895

How Whites Smoke Opium in Chinatown

Haunts of "Hop Heads" in the Mongolian Quarter

MANY DENS ARE OPEN

Blind Annie's "Joint" on Jackson Street Frequented by Girls and Men

IN DEFIANCE OF THE LAWS

The Veil Slightly Drawn From Some of the Worst Resorts in San Francisco

I.

EXTENT OF THE OPIUM TRAFFIC. ONLY A PLAIN STATEMENT OF FACTS.

Notwithstanding a keen public sentiment in this City against the abuse of the opium traffic, in spite of stringent state and municipal laws forbidding and restricting the use of the drug, there are about 3000

How Whites Smoke Opium in Chinatown

"fiends" or "hop heads" in San Francisco; the number is constantly on the increase; there are over 300 "joints," dens, rooms and lodging-houses, inside and outside of Chinatown, where the "habit" may be indulged with impunity, and perhaps a score of places where "dope" is sold illicitly.

These statements are made advisedly and only after considerable investigation. A great deal has been written about the opium "fiends" of San Francisco, but the subject has hitherto been usually handled from its darkly picturesque side. The generalities have, in the aggregate and in their conclusions, been true enough, but specific information has been lacking.

It is difficult to overdraw the black miseries of the lives of the opium "fiends," or to understate the moral and physical dangers to the community of this horrible traffic in the drug. But in the present instance The Call's purpose is to state facts concerning the odious traffic rather than conclusions or moral abstractions on its influence. The facts have been difficult to secure, because no assistance was sought or obtained from the police department. A bare recital of how the facts were finally obtained would be interesting, not to say spicy, reading for the public at large and for several individuals in particular. But this is not to be a spicy story, and is interesting only inasmuch as a sober statement of somber and sorrowful facts may be.

And the facts are given for the good they may do; for the lessons they may bear to those whose duty it is to enforce the laws against the illegal trade in opium and the maintenance of opium joints and dens. Not all the facts are given, nor even the worst of them. The whole case is not stated; could not be stated in anything less than a book of many pages. Only that which is fit for popular reading is published. There is much more to be seen and learned by one who would follow the dark tale to its dregs; but to see them and know them one must, for the time being, become himself a part of this worst and lowest phase of the slums of San Francisco.

II.

STATE AND MUNICIPAL LAWS
RESTRICTING AND FORBIDDING THE VICIOUS TRAFFIC

As in the case of many other evils it can scarcely be urged by the authorities that the laws and ordinances against the opium traffic are not stringent enough or that their wording is uncertain. Section 307 of the Penal Code of California, in effect since March, 1881, is very plain spoken, as follows: Every person who opens or "maintains, to be resorted to by other persons, any place where opium, or any of its preparations, is sold or given away, to be smoked at such place, and any person who at such place sells or gives away any opium, or its said preparations, to be there smoked or otherwise used, and every person who visits or resorts to any such place for the purpose of smoking opium, or its said preparations, is guilty of a misdemeanor, and upon conviction thereof shall be punished by a fine not exceeding five hundred dollars or imprisonment in the County Jail not exceeding six months, or by both such fine and imprisonment." In pursuance with the provisions of the State law and to further restrict the opium evil that was introduced and is chiefly carried on in San Francisco by the Chinese the Board of Supervisors in 1890 amended order 1587 by section 61, which reads as follows: "No person shall, in the City and County of San Francisco, keep or maintain, or become an inmate of, or visit, or shall in any way contribute to the support of, any place, house or room where opium is smoked, or where persons assemble for the purpose of smoking opium, or inhaling the fumes of opium. Any person violating any of the provisions of this section shall be deemed guilty of a misdemeanor and on conviction thereof be punished by a fine not less than $250 nor more than $1000, or by imprisonment not less than three months or more than six months, or by both such fine and imprisonment."

There are still other ordinances and laws restricting the opium traffic. Order 2085, passed in 1889, prohibits any person whatever from selling or giving or exchanging opium in any form except upon the presentation by the purchaser of a bona-fide physician's prescription of the same date upon which the purchase is made. They are all broken constantly and in many quarters of the city, but the state law and the municipal order forbidding the keeping or frequenting of houses or rooms where opium may be smoked are those most frequently and flagrantly violated.

Reporting: Immigrants 1803-1931

III.

A LIST OF CHINESE "JOINTS" FREQUENTED BY THE "HOP HEADS"

The following list of the places where the so-called "hop heads" or opium "fiends" rendezvous to satisfy or palliate their depraved craving for the "habit," and where the uninitiated, if he or she be properly vouched for or chaperoned, may learn to use the drug, is by no means complete. It is correct, however, and proves the "joints" to be sufficiently numerous to show that the policemen in these districts are not as vigilant as they should be—and this is stating it mildly.

The "joints" where the Chinese may and do smoke opium are almost innumerable, far too numerous, in fact, and much too open and well known or easily discoverable to need designation at this time. They are, of course, illegal, since the law makes no distinction in race and color. But the resorts in Chinatown where whites may and do smoke opium—that is another matter, the matter under consideration here.

The following is a list of the "joints" in Chinatown frequented by whites who go there to smoke opium:

BLIND ANNIE'S CELLAR, entrance through the passageway between 718 and 720 Jackson street. Resort for white girls. Supposed to be under the protection of the police.

AH KING'S JOINT, entrance by a narrow and steep flight of stairs at 620 Jackson street. The most notorious resort for whites in Chinatown.

HOP JAY, in the rear of 730 Jackson street. Known as the "Palace Hotel" of Chinatown. Second floor. Also a "joint" in same building on the third floor.

39 WAVERLEY PLACE, entrance south of the barber-shop. In third story attic.

116 WAVERLEY PLACE, double yellow doors, entrance to the north. Second story, rear.

SANG JO HE, entrance between 921 and 923 Dupont street. Second story, rear.

17 WASHINGTON ALLEY (known as Fish alley), a passageway that leads through to Dupont street. There are several "joints" here.

DUNCOMBE ALLEY, a narrow causeway that runs from Jackson to Pacific street. There are no numbers, but in the middle of the alley, on the west side, is an entrance that leads to a room frequented by whites.

812 CLAY STREET, second story in the rear.

AH SING, 834-1/2 Washington street, entrance through a tobacco-store. Third story front. White girls and men.

CHURCH ALLEY, about the center of the block, entrance through deserted gambling-rooms to two joints on west side.

809 STOCKTON STREET, between Sacramento and Clay. Big brick building containing several resorts run by a Chinese. Opposite the consulate.

1009 STOCKTON STREET, third floor.

1023 STOCKTON STREET, the old McKenzie building, first and second floors. Notorious. White women and children found there at all hours.

AH KING, 720 Jackson street, rear.

835 JACKSON, run by a Chinese doctor.

7-1/2 WAVERLY PLACE, in basement.

AH SUEY, first floor, 834 Clay street.

AH SING, Second floor, 834 Clay street.

How Whites Smoke Opium in Chinatown

IV.

THE POPULAR LAWMAKER
AND THE GLASSY-EYED "HOP HEAD"

Starting in on the task to expose something of the extent of the illicit opium traffic in San Francisco, with the injunction to procure facts instead of general material, was a most difficult thing for one who knew little or nothing of the ways and the haunts of the victims of the "habit," known in the vernacular as "hop heads" or "fiends."

Certain Chinatown guides were tried first. These led the way to Blind Annie's famous "joint"—but always at a time when no white girls or men were smoking there—and to many of the Chinese opium "joints" already enumerated. But always only Chinese would be found smoking. The guides took good care that no white people should be shown in the act of "hitting the pipe."

When asked to be taken where the whites smoked opium the guides declared there were no such places; that the law was very strict, and the police kept such close watch that neither inside nor outside of the Chinese quarter could there be found places where white men and women inhaled the drug.

A lawyer's assistant, who knows every corner and alley in Chinatown and the tenderloin districts nearby, was next appealed to for the desired information. He frankly admitted that the white "joints" were numerous and the "hop heads" almost without number—but—

His "but" was that he found these people very useful at election time, and therefore he must not endanger their friendship and allegiance by betraying their haunts. Other methods were tried— many others. "Hop heads" were followed, sometimes paid for leading the way to their rendezvous. This was a slow and unsatisfactory process. Sometimes two or three "fiends" would lead all to the same building. By three different persons the way was shown to the lodging-house at 633 California street. Two of the informants were women, who went there to smoke in a fiend's room.

And many of the "fiends" that were followed refused to betray their haunts and comrades. Many of them are well dressed and are not to be tempted by any moderate sum of money. These are the men who live off the earnings of fallen women. Some of them have diamonds in their shirt fronts. They are known on the streets as "dude fiends." That they are victims of the seductive and degrading drug one can easily see. All are thin, pale and glassy-eyed. These are three unfailing signs borne by every man or woman who has a regular "habit."

At last, through the kindly offices of a popular and well-known south of Market street lawmaker, who knew a man who knew another man who, for a sufficient consideration, would undertake to show two Eastern tourists something of life among the opium-smokers in San Francisco, acquaintances were established that led to the knowledge, only a portion of which is now published.

It is a fact that the opium dens of this city are not easy of access, but it is also true that they are carried on under the very eyes of the policemen in certain quarters of the city. On two different occasions policemen were seen to enter these resorts and remain there for some time.

Yet however difficult it is for a stranger to open the doors of an opium joint, and however difficult it may or may not be for the policemen on the respective beats to discover their whereabouts, a great many young men and women from respectable homes find it all too easy to force an entrance. Almost anyone can gain evidence of the truth of this assertion by noting that the houses named are frequented by young people in all stages of the "habit." Some are learning, for one must smoke many times before the system becomes thoroughly inoculated and indulgence is not followed by nausea. Some smoke once a day, some twice and some three times a day. But once even a "mild habit" is formed there is no longer any hope for the victim. Once a "fiend" always a "fiend," is a commonplace expression among the "hop heads."

V.

INTERIOR VIEWS OF SOME OF THE CHINATOWN OPIUM DENS

One of the most valuable acquaintances formed through the medium of the "well known and popular lawmaker" was that of a young man who has what he calls a "twenty-cent habit." This means that he smokes 20 cents' worth of opium a day, or one li gee. The latter designation describes to Asiatic ears a Chinese nutshell about the size of a beechnut, filled with first-class opium. The li gee is sold in many places in Chinatown. You can watch the "fiends" coming north on Dupont street every night for their li gees. If you follow them you can easily guess where they buy.

This young man with the "twenty-cent habit"— tall, stoop-shouldered, painfully thin and glassy-eyed— was invaluable in Chinatown.

"Do you know that Blind Annie's cellar is a resort for white girls?" was the first information he gave.

Everybody who visits Chinatown has seen Blind Annie and her cats, yet only the initiate know about the white girls frequenting her dingy cellar. To reach it you enter the first dark alley that leads north off Jackson street, above Kearny. When you reach the end of the alley you come upon a courtyard and a foul smell. The courtyard has balconies all around it and for three stories above the street. You go down a few steps and then turn to the left to reach Blind Annie.

You cannot push open her door with impunity, for it is usually locked. The guide always knocks and sometimes does not gain admission.

It was midnight when The Call man and the young man with the "twenty-cent habit" knocked on Annie's door.

"You stand to one side," said the guide to the other. Then the guide parleyed a while with Annie and assured her that his friends (Eastern tourists) were all right. Just what passed between the two a Caucasian uneducated in the Chinese tongue will never know, but it was sufficient to gain an admittance for all three.

There were four other white people in Annie's place. Two were women — evil looking women, though still young. All four were smoking and Annie was fondling her cats.

Blind Annie's room has a superficial area of perhaps 120 square feet. When the door is shut, as it must be when she has white smokers, there is not a particle of ventilation unless it is from the cracks around the door. The atmosphere was stifling with the fumes of the drug that came from the four pipes and it was scarcely safe for one unused to inhaling the smoke to remain in the room many minutes.

The room is foul and dirty. Blind Annie sits in the corner on a mat that is greasy and elevated from the floor about two feet. If she tried to stand straight in her bunk her head would bang against the upper bunk before she was half straightened out—and Annie is a small creature. On the opposite side of the room there are similar tiers of bunks. Each bunk has two square Chinese mats and on every mat is a "dope" layout—a tray, a nut-oil lamp, a small box of the brown and sticky drug, a vessel for ashes, a needle with which to cook and manipulate the stuff and the bamboo pipe.

Blind Annie's fee is graded according to the "habit" of the smoker. For two bits a very big "habit" can be satisfied for the time being—an indulgence of from thirty to thirty-five small pills. And this is the kind of "habit" those who frequent Annie's joint usually suffer from. It is a "big habit" in the vernacular of the "fiends." One must have courted the vice assiduously or have been smoking many years to have cultivated such a "habit."

"I never smoke more than twenty pills at a time," said one of the young women who was induced to show the visitors how to smoke. "That isn't enough to put me under the influence, but it braces me up after a hard day, and that's all I care about.

"Oh, it would soon grow if I'd let it, but I'm not going to be a 'fiend.' I've hit the pipe these five years now and am not a 'fiend' yet. You don't catch this girl getting to be a 'hophead.'"

This appears to be a popular hallucination with the victims of the opium habit—everyone knows the other is a fiend, but thinks himself or herself only a dilettanti in the vice. But the glassy eyes and shrunken frame tell their own story.

Carrie was the name of the girl who volunteered the information about herself. She kept on rolling the pills and puffing the smoke. "This is the twelfth," she said, as she laid back on the box that served for a pillow, and drew in the seductive fumes of the brown, sizzling little pill. Presently, when the twentieth pill had been burned to ashes, Carrie's head sank back on the box and her eyes were heavy.

"Guess I've taken a bit too much this time," she said. "I'll sleep it off a bit before I go."

"She's good till morning," said the guide. "She has the desired effect now, sure. She always talks that way about taking a little too much, but she never quits till the sleep comes on."

Carrie was the first of the patrons of Annie that night to receive the "desired effect"— as the simon-pure Chinatown guide always calls it. The others were in various stages of indulgence. Annie stroked the kittens beside her and crooned. When the customary nickels were dropped on the tray in front of her by the visitors she said "Tanks" quite plainly.

How Whites Smoke Opium in Chinatown

"Didn't the gentlemen want to smoke?" she asked the guide in her native tongue. They did not.

Ah Sing's joint, on the top floor of 834 Washington street, was the next place visited that night. The entrance is through a small tobacco-store kept by Chinese. When you reach the landing at the head of the first flight you find a narrow courtyard with balconies at each story. You turn to the right and go up still another flight of dark stairs. Then a little to the left, and the first door you come to is Ah Sing's. His room is a trifle larger than Annie's, and there are only two big bunks in it, one on each side. He has an assistant of his own race, and the two of them wait on their customers assiduously. There were three of the latter stretched out on the bunks, and one of these had already secured the "desired effect."

"He's only been smoking about a month, and a half dozen pills sets him off," explained the guide, who recognized the slumberer.

Ah Sing was careful to lock the door after his visitor had been admitted. He was surprised when he found they did not want to smoke, but he accepted the two 25 cent pieces tendered him with becoming Mongolian meekness and thankfulness.

The other Chinese joints visited were about the same. The layout is the same. There is always a hop tray of "dope" in front of the reclining smoker; the nut-oil lamp (the dong) for cooking; the hank or needle with which the ah pin yin (opium) is manipulated, and the big jin ten, or bamboo pipe.

In one night six places in Chinatown were visited, and at every place white men and women were found smoking. Another night four joints were entered by the white tourists, and in all of them whites were smoking and the visitors were offered the privilege of "hitting the pipe" for the small fee of 15 cents.

Though it was not easy for a novice to find these places it seems strange that the trained policemen and detectives, with every resource at their command, cannot discover their whereabouts. Indeed, it is said that the police do know the location of these and many other dens. It is said, too, that the police wink—but, then, this is a narration of fact, not of hearsay.

These are the facts regarding Chinatown. If the police have been in ignorance of these dens, as Chief Crowley has declared himself to be, at least they need be no longer in ignorance.

San Francisco Call
April 29, 1899

Huntington and Schwerin Employ Washington Lobbyists to Protect the Dishonest Chinese Passenger Traffic of the Pacific Mail

Dispatches received from Washington last night throw a new and startling light upon the secret causes of the dismissal of R. E. Meredith as chief of the Chinese Bureau of this city. Meredith was discharged from his position of trust for cause. The Call, in its endeavor to remedy the glaring abuses of the Chinese Bureau, exposed the methods of Meredith, and today it will expose the powerful corporations which stood sponsor for Meredith in his manipulations. The Chinese Bureau of this city is the only practical barrier on the Pacific Coast to the uninterrupted influx of Chinese coolies to the United States.

The officers of the bureau are expected to be honest, efficient and vigilant. In their hands rests the vitally important duty of enforcing the exclusion act and of preventing the degraded laborers of the Orient from entering the port of San Francisco. Meredith, the chief of the bureau, was dismissed from the service of the Federal Government because he was found grossly negligent of his sworn duties.

The Call will show today that the Southern Pacific Company, C. P. Huntington, the Pacific Mail Steamship Company and R. P. Schwerin were the supporters and sponsors of Meredith, his close friends while in office and his persistent defenders while in disgrace. The officers of the Southern Pacific Company and of the Pacific Mail Steamship Company exercised every influence within their power to restore Meredith to his position after he had been discharged.

They appealed to John P. Jackson, Collector of the Port, and secured his unqualified endorsement of Meredith, in character and ability. An effort was made at Washington to induce the Secretary of the Treasury to reconsider his decision of dismissal. Paid lobbyists of the Southern Pacific Company and of the Pacific Mail Steamship Company were ordered to use their seductive arts upon federal officials at Washington and if possible save Meredith from dismissal. An appeal was even made to President

McKinley himself to save from final discharge this officer whose duty it was to keep Chinese out and not to let them in.

The cause of this campaign to save a petty official from dismissal, the motives of telegrams, letters and vehement personal instruction might, by a stretch of the imagination, be a mystery. But R. P. Schwerin, the protege and beneficiary of the bounty of C. P. Huntington, gives the reason. The Pacific Mail Steamship Company profits by the illegitimate traffic in Chinese coolies. It reaps an ill-gotten harvest in freights and fares from coolies that by legislative enactment are barred from an entrance into the United States.

Every Chinese who is brought from China to this port and is then denied a landing becomes a burden upon the Pacific Mail. Every Chinese who comes and, rightly or wrongly, is permitted to enter is an element of profit to the corrupt corporation that lives to make money at whatever cost to the people it preys upon. The Pacific Mail Steamship Company has been and is involved in an illegitimate Chinese traffic. Any measure which interferes with that traffic is, to the officers of the Pacific Mail, an affront and a trespass upon their vicious rights. And when B. E. Meredith was removed from his position as chief of the Chinese Bureau R. P. Schwerin wrote to C. P. Huntington in New York:

"You must have Meredith reinstated. His removal means a body blow at the Chinese passenger traffic of the Pacific Mail Company."

And C P. Huntington replied:

"I will do all I can."

And C. P. Huntington did all he could to save the Chinese passenger traffic of the Pacific Mail. He had advocated Chinese immigration before and after the United States government prohibited this terrible influx of coolies into American territory. He had championed the cause of degraded hordes of cheap laborers because that cause meant profit to him. He had used his steamship line as a vehicle with which to cheat federal laws and injure American workingmen. When his lieutenant sounded the alarm, C. P. Huntington needed no second warning. He at once communicated with his agents at Washington.

Letters between Huntington and Schwerin passed in quick succession. The wires were laid and Huntington soon issued his orders to David A. Chambers, one of the paid "attorneys" of the Southern Pacific company at Washington. Mr. Chambers was not slow to act, and in the following dispatch he tells what he did and how he tried to save B. E. Meredith from the ax of official decapitation:

"WASHINGTON, April 28—David A. Chambers, who is the regular Washington attorney for the Southern Pacific company in all land matters, was asked today if he was interested in having Meredith reinstated as inspector and chief of the Chinese Bureau. He replied:

"Several weeks ago I received a letter from our people saying that Meredith was a good man; that he had been highly recommended by Collector Jackson and should be restored. I went to see Assistant Secretary Howell, who explained that Meredith had been found guilty of negligence and collusion in allowing Fong Suey Wan to escape when she should have been held as a procuress and therefore Howell emphatically declined to take any further action in the case."

"By 'our people' do you refer to Southern Pacific officers?" inquired The Call correspondent.

"Yes," replied Mr. Chambers. "I wrote them that nothing could be done for Meredith."

The Treasury Department expects J. R. Dunn to arrive in San Francisco in a day or two to take charge of the Chinese Bureau, vacated by Meredith. Collector Jackson will not have supervision over it as reported some time ago.

The foregoing dispatch is doubly significant. It shows that the Southern Company and the Pacific Mail, allied powers of corruption, are engaged in using their tremendous power to defeat the purpose of the exclusion act and to flood the country with coolie laborers. The dispatch shows also that Collector Jackson will have nothing to do with the administration of a department that has been frequently sullied by scandal and mismanagement since its establishment. The history of Meredith's regime in the Chinese Bureau may indicate in a measure why C. P. Huntington and R. P. Schwerin were so anxious to have him retained in office.

The final turning down of Meredith and his backers, the Pacific Mail Steamship Company, collector Jackson and other of kindred sentiment by the Secretary of the Treasury, will be hailed with delight by all the friends of labor in the United States, particularly on the Pacific Coast. During the period of two years in which the affairs of the Chinese Bureau were "managed" by Meredith and Jackson the number of Chinese immigrants, including those returning to this State, jumped to a figure more than double that under Wise's administration, even when Dick Williams stood at the gates and made a fortune for himself and his pals out of the business of being a member of the Chinese Bureau.

It is noteworthy that about the first official act of Customs Collector Jackson on assuming his office was the announcement to the members of the press that he had confirmed Mr. Wise's appointment of R. E. Meredith as chief of the Chinese Bureau. And it is equally noteworthy that during the two years of Mr. Jackson's administration of the Chinese Bureau Mr. Schwerin and the other officials and friends of the Pacific Mail Steamship Company felicitated themselves when they read in the daily papers that the number of Chinese immigrants arriving and settling in California had increased from 1700 annually, which was the number under the Wise administration, to 3500 annually under the Jackson-Meredith administration. It is a fact equally noteworthy that since the Secretary of the Treasury kicked Meredith out of office, the business of the Chinese brokers has fallen away to a minimum.

Certain lawyers who almost made the bureau their home when Mr. Meredith was there have disappeared from the Appraisers' building and are looking for Caucasian clients. Certain attachés of other offices in the same building who were wont to go into the vault and examine papers in Chinese cases every day are now conspicuous by the rarity of their presence. The lodgings maintained by the steamship company in the Mail Dock for housing Chinese immigrants awaiting a landing are no longer overcrowded, and the abuse of keeping those unfortunate creatures six months on the dock before being granted a hearing has been stopped. But it is noteworthy, also, that the abuse was not abated by any initiatory step taken by Jackson or his friend Meredith. It was done at the suggestion of Special Agents Linck and Smith, who, when they arrived here and looked into the matter of the gross mismanagement of the Chinese Bureau, made such representations as to bring about a general and speedy clearing up of the Mongolian debris.

The laborers of California owe a debt of gratitude to the firmness and clear-sightedness of the Secretary of the Treasury, who refused to be influenced by a great corporation and who was too shrewd to be misled by the lies told both here and in Washington in Meredith's behalf to waver for an instant in adopting heroic measures to protect the people of the United States from this flood of yellow paupers coming in through the Golden Gate at the rate of nearly 4000 per annum. The first of these measures and one that brought consternation to the coolie brokers was the appointment of Chinese Interpreter Rev. John Endicott Gardiner, D. D., as a Chinese inspector. Gardiner was the last man in the world that Jackson or Meredith wanted to see in the bureau. Meredith had spoken in the most contemptuous manner about him and to him on one occasion threatening physically to kick him out of the office. Jackson was known to have a disparaging opinion of the reverend gentleman also. Inspector Lynch was equally disliked by Meredith, and although Lynch and Gardiner had been the two most active and successful members of the bureau, Jackson refused to appoint either one to the head of the bureau when the place was vacated. The cold shoulder extended to the inspectors named might be interpreted, in the absence of a more plausible theory, as an intimation that virtue was to be its own sweet solitary reward in the bureau. In other words, that Gardiner and Lynch had got themselves disliked because they were too zealous in the discharge of their duties.

Hence the totally unexpected appointment of Dr. Gardiner to a position where he would be untrammeled in the discharge of those duties with which he had been entrusted was a bitter dose for the coolie ring. It also revealed the seriously alarming fact that the Secretary of the Treasury was fully informed of the mismanagement of the bureau, and that he had resolved to put an end to it, no matter whether a major or a general was to be displaced thereby. The fact also that the appointment was made without consulting either Jackson or Meredith, or asking them for a letter of recommendation, was another disagreeable element of the episode. This was followed shortly after by the appointment by the Secretary of Chinese Inspectors Tippitt and Barbour, sent from the East to become members of the bureau at San Francisco. In the selection of these three men the Collector and Meredith had no voice whatever. They had to accept what they received in a spirit of resignation or indignation, whichever suited best their official moods, and no vote of thanks has yet appeared on record for the same.

But the hardest blow of all was the appointment of James R. Dunn as chief of the bureau without previous notice to the Collector. More than that, the fact of the appointment was known to the Washington correspondent of The Call and was announced in the columns of The Call long before Collector Jackson admitted that he had heard anything at all about it. These acts on the part of the Treasury Department are susceptible of only one interpretation, and that is that the department has determined to manage the bureau from Washington and in its own way, the bureau to be independent of the Collector, and the bureau and the Collector being a check upon the lapses and errors of each other. Furthermore, that the department will not tolerate the methods heretofore pursued in the bureau which permitted that office to be made the rendezvous for Chinese brokers and their attorneys.

It is understood that Customs Surveyor Spear, who has charge of the immigrants on the Mail dock, will be allowed to prevent gangs of highbinders from visiting the immigrants and scheming with them to secure their illegal landing in this State. It will be remembered by The Call's readers that about the middle of last September Surveyor Spear issued an order to the customs inspectors at the gate that no permit to visit the Chinese on board the steamer or on the dock should be recognized unless countersigned by himself. This action was taken by the Surveyor in order to stop a grave abuse of the visiting privilege, whereby the efforts of honest officials to prevent the illegal importation of coolies was thwarted. For instance Mr. Spear came into possession of passes issued by Meredith for four persons to visit one immigrant—two white men and two Chinamen. When Collector Jackson's attention was called to the matter he said that the permit was proper, the four persons being no doubt the white lawyer, the Chinese client, the Chinese interpreter and a white photographer. On the very next day Mr. Jackson issued an order proclaiming: that no permits should be recognized, except such as bore the signature of Meredith, thus nullifying the order issued by Mr. Spear and leaving the management of the detained Chinese in the hands of Meredith. When the Collector was asked why he had practically revoked the order issued by Mr. Spear he replied that he, the Collector, was the person designated by law to handle the Chinese, and that Spear had no authority in the premises. Yet it is the fact that Mr. Spear always has had custody of the Chinese at the Mail Dock by virtue of his official position and still exercises the function of jailer.

It is understood that under the new method of conducting the bureau, a Chinese interpreter in the service of the government will be present at every interview with a Chinese immigrant seeking to land and that highbinders and coolie brokers will be no longer allowed to ply their nefarious avocation under the noses of the federal officials. Mr. Spear, who is responsible for the safe keeping of the Chinese prisoners at the Mail

Dock, will be allowed to take such measures as he may deem necessary to ensure their detention until legally landed.

Much good will be accomplished by the new mode of enforcing the exclusion act. The head of the bureau will no longer be the creature of the Collector, and will be therefore more independent in the performance of his duties. He will be directly responsible to the Secretary of the Treasury for whatever mistakes he may make, and there will be no collectors and ex-collectors to intercede for him and furnish certificates of character to save him from the departmental wrath. He must stand upon his own feet, and his character must speak, not through hearsay certificates, but through his official acts. The trouble with Meredith has been that his certificates of character don't dovetail with his official mistakes which, unfortunately for him, if they were mistakes, were on the wrong side. They were invariably on the side of the Pacific Mail Steamship Company and the slave dealers and against the interests of the exclusion act and the government. No merchant will keep a clerk who makes mistakes in giving change against his employer or who doles out good coins for counterfeit.

Again, if, after Mr. Jackson shall have retired from office to rest upon such laurels as he may have won, a bad man, working in the interest of the Pacific Mail Steamship Company, should receive the appointment as Collector of the Port, the head of the Chinese Bureau will be an eye of the government glaring upon him. If he allows a Chinaman to enter without being entitled to the privilege, the Chinaman will be arrested and the act of the Collector will be reviewed by the bureau and the court. Thus there will be an effectual check upon the Collector; and on the other hand, if the Pacific Mail Steamship Company shall foist into the bureau another Meredith, the Collector may act as a check upon the chief, and may take such measures as may be calculated to expose and punish fraud or criminal mistakes.

Consistently with their past record of mendacity and low cunning, Meredith and his backers have made use of misrepresentation and prevarication in their unsuccessful and shameless effort to have him reinstated into his old position as chief of the Chinese Bureau. They have circulated a report that he was dismissed, not because of any neglect of duty, but because he used insulting language to a reporter of The Call and to Dr. Gardiner. They argued both orally and on paper (from the office of the Pacific Mail Steamship Company) that his offense arose from great provocation and that, after all, all that he was guilty of was giving way to his temper. He was not dismissed because Fong Suey Wan escaped, they said, and the assertion that her escape was the cause of his dismissal they declared to be an oral slander and a printed libel. A letter written by Collector Jackson and exhibited by Meredith's friends is so worded as to befog the subject. The circulation of such false statements is not calculated to do the Pacific Mail Steamship Company any good, for the Secretary of the Treasury knows why Meredith was let go. In order to set the matter right, it is necessary to recapitulate briefly the nature of the investigation which resulted in the recent upheaval in the bureau for the good of the service.

An exposition was held last summer in Omaha and among the concessions was one of the Mee Lee Village Association, a Chinese company, which reproduced a Chinese village on the grounds and gave theatrical and acrobatic entertainments. About five hundred men and women of more or less—generally less—virtue were imported from China to take part in the village show, and they were admitted under a special privilege granted by the United States, under the terms of which the actors, acrobats, shopkeepers and attendants were to return to China at the expiration of three months after the close of the exposition.

It was found that before the exposition closed about 200 women, mostly of the boatmen's class, had left Omaha and had gone to reside in different cities in the Union, San Francisco getting the most of them. This becoming known, the government ordered Major Moore to organize a raid upon the Chinatown bagnios in this city for the purpose of arresting and deporting the runaways. Collector Jackson detailed a large force of customs inspectors to assist in the raid, but for some reason never made public the police were informed of the contemplated movement and were stationed in the houses to be raided, where they were found a half-hour later by the Federal posse in full possession and the whole of Chinatown advised of what was going on. The Federal posse were detained at the Custom House awaiting the order of Jackson to start.

Notwithstanding the publicity given to the affair about twenty-seven women without certificates were captured. Among the number taken to the Presbyterian Chinese Mission on Sacramento street was a middle-aged woman named Fong Suey Wan, a notorious procuress of considerable wealth and the wife of the partner of Little Pete, a noted Chinese boss and slave dealer, lately deceased by the grace of a highbinder's bullet in a Chinatown barber shop. When the women were being questioned at the mission Miss Cameron, the matron, recognized the procuress and informed Meredith of her identity. Meredith ordered her to be detained notwithstanding that her certificate in due form was then being presented for inspection.

Nothing further was done by Meredith to hold the woman. He filed no complaint against her, he did not even inform the United States Marshal, the District Attorney or anyone else in authority that he proposed to place any charge against her. On the next day after her arrest Arthur Lotto, a reporter, warned Meredith that the woman would be discharged on presentation of her certificate before Court Commissioner Heacock if Meredith did not file a complaint charging her with being a procuress. Meredith replied that it was "all right," he was getting up "a great case" against her. On the next morning the woman was taken before Commissioner Heacock, on the same floor as the Chinese Bureau and about seventy-five feet distant, and her certificate being produced, the court stated that he would recommend her discharge, there being no complaint accusing her of any offense. She was then taken to the office of the United States Marshal, directly underneath the office of the Chinese Bureau, and kept there until 2 o'clock in the afternoon, when she was brought before United States District Judge de Haven and discharged. Then she disappeared.

Meredith could offer no reasonable explanation as to why he had allowed the woman to escape, and public clamor was raised, the episode savoring too strongly of corruption to be passed by in silence. Special Agent Moore, in pursuance of instructions from Washington, made an investigation, examining witnesses and taking affidavits of all parties concerned. He sent his report to Washington, and about the time that the department was looking into the report ex-Collector Wise appeared in Washington and told the Treasury people and the newspaper correspondents a fairy story to the effect that the woman was allowed to go because Major Moore and Miss Cameron had asked that Fong Suey be allowed to return to China.

As a matter of justice to Mr. Wise it must be said that he knew nothing of the case of his own knowledge, as all his information had been derived from Meredith and his friends. Then charges were filed against Special Agent Moore for making an assault upon a woman employed in his office as typewriter, and the Secretary of the Treasury, in view of Moore's disgrace, sent Moore's report back to this city to be verified by

Special Agents Linck and Smith. The witnesses were re-examined and the Fong Suey Wan report was sent on to Washington once more. It was upon this report, which dealt with the Fong Suey Wan incident alone, that Meredith was dismissed. Subsequently the special agents sent a supplemental report to Washington in connection with the matter of Meredith having used abusive language to Dr. Gardiner and a reporter of The Call, but before it had reached the Secretary of the Treasury Meredith had been dismissed from the service. That is why Meredith's application for reinstatement was found to have no force, for he utterly failed to show that he was innocent of the charge of having allowed the noted procuress to walk out of his hands.

Pacific Commercial Advertiser
August 22, 1899

Italian Laborers

Experience on Louisiana Plantations

The Only Race That Can Successfully Compete With Negroes In Semi-Tropical Climes

NEW ORLEANS, August 1. The lynching of the five Italians at Tallulah, La., and the ordering away of the other Italians in Madison parish may temporarily check the Italian immigration into North Louisiana and thereby interrupt a movement which is having an extraordinary influence on Louisiana and promises to hasten a solution of the color, or race, question. The interruption, though, is likely to be only temporary.

The Italians seem to be the only race that can labor successfully and compete with the negro in the semi-tropical climate of Louisiana. They have been arriving for the last twenty years at the rate of many thousands each year, and the census soon to be taken will show that largely because of this immigration districts and parishes which formerly had a large majority of negroes are now white. Among these are Plaquemine, Assumption, Terrebonne, Iberia and St. John. The Italian immigration has naturally been largest in southern Louisiana in the territory around New Orleans, where there is already a large Latin population. Thence it has spread into the northern parishes, where it has met with a far from hearty welcome; but the Italians seem to have the patience and perseverance of the Chinese, enduring persecution and overcoming prejudice by mere persistence.

No better evidence could be presented of this triumph over bitter prejudice than is found right here in New Orleans. The parish prison lynching of eight years ago was a blow from which many thought the Italian colony of New Orleans would never recover. Perhaps 6,000 or 8,000 Italians left New Orleans then, seeing no hope or future for themselves here, and settled in Memphis, St. Louis, Chicago and at other points. But the Italians have lived down the Hennessy assassination and the discredit of the Mafia, and have more than regained their former position. The Italian colony of New Orleans has doubled in numbers since the parish prison lynching affair, and in wealth and standing has advanced far more. It has taken the first place among the foreign population of New Orleans. There are now two daily Italian papers in New Orleans, and Signor Enrico Cavalli, the editor of one of them, the Italo-Americano, is the representative appointed by the Italian government to investigate the Tallulah lynching. Schools have been established, at which the Italians are taught not only English but their mother tongue, and King Humbert, through the Italian Consul, has contributed liberally to the support of these schools, which keep alive a love for Italy in the hearts of its sons.

The status of the Italians has been very much improved of late; they dropped the hand organ long ago, and they never took to barbering, shoe-cleaning or street work, as in New York. From cobbling they have better branched out into the manufacture of shoes, and they control some of the largest factories in the South. The fruit, vegetable and fish trades they have absolutely controlled since they first came, for they are without rivals in peddling. They are rapidly crowding into the corner grocery business, formerly monopolized by Irishmen and Germans, and into nearly all lines, even the learned professions. Latterly they have been quite conspicuous in politics.

It is, however, in the country districts that the Italians are making themselves most felt. Three-fourths of the Italian immigrants are from Naples or Sicily. They are peasants, accustomed to farm work, and they

Italian Laborers

come over here to work on the sugar plantations. They come from limited areas even in Sicily and Naples. The little town of Contessa Entellina, for instance, has more of its citizens in Louisiana than at home; and Cefalu, from which came all the men lynched in Madison parish the other day, has several thousand of its sons and daughters in Louisiana. The immigrants are with rare exceptions a hardy, robust race, willing to work and impervious to the climate. The Immigration Commissioner at this port declares that the character of the Italians arriving is steadily improving. They find work the day they arrive. Some come over in the summer, work through the grinding season, when wages are high, and return to Italy in the winter with their earnings; but this practice is dying out and a majority of the immigrants come to stay, learn English, or something like English, as soon as they can, and apply for naturalization papers. Not a few adopt English names like Brown, Smith or Jones, in order to be thorough Americans. They doff their picturesque costumes within a week of their arrival and pick up a cheap imitation of American dress.

They make good laborers and give Italian perfect satisfaction to the planters, being infinitely superior to the negroes. The Louisiana planters have been for years trying to get some substitute for the negroes, who are not trustworthy. The Italians come nearest to fulfilling all conditions. They are well satisfied with their wages and save money where the negro cannot. They do not drink, and cause little trouble. They are willing to live in the same cabins as the negroes and to work with them in the fields on equal terms, and they work hard and faithfully. They have, therefore, given satisfaction and are rapidly crowding the negro back from the sugar district. In all the districts immediately around New Orleans, where the negro furnished nine-tenths of the labor ten years ago, the Italians are in a majority today. New Orleans was a white oasis in the midst of a population overwhelmingly negro at the last census; the new enumeration will show that Plaquemine and St. Bernard below, Jefferson and St. John above, Terrebonne, Lafourche, Iberia and St. Martin's on the west have become white; that is, have a majority of white population thanks to the immigration of the Italians and the rapid increase of the Acadians (brethren of Evangeline), the two races which are doing the most to support the Southern theory of "white supremacy," but who are looked down on with contempt by the Americans, the Creoles and the other white races.

Reporting: Immigrants 1803-1931

The position of the Italian in Louisiana is very anomalous because of the race, or, rather, the negro, question. Neither the whites nor the negroes know how to class him he is, as it were, a link connecting the white and black races. Swarthy in color, the Sicilians are darker than the griffes and quadroons, the negro half-breeds of southern Louisiana, but they are undoubtedly white. On the other hand, they are willing to live in the same quarters with the negroes and to work side by side with them, and seem wholly destitute of that anti-negro prejudice which is one of the distinguishing features of all the white races in the South. It cannot be said that this attitude of the Sicilians toward the negro has won his gratitude. He looks upon the Italian with pretty much the same feeling as he entertained of old toward the poor white trash. He has no respect for the Italian and refuses to treat him with the respect and deference shown to other white men. He will not take off his hat to him or call him "Mister," a word which is never applied under any circumstances to the negro in the South, even when Colonel and Judge are used, and which the negro always uses of the whites.

It is the same with the whites. The average man will classify the population as whites, dagoes and negroes. This is the explanation of the lynching of Italians in Louisiana. Not 99 per cent but 100 per cent of the white men lynched in this State have been Italians. There have been wholesale Italian lynchings in New Orleans, St. Charles, St. John and Madison. The unwritten law of the South is that a white man shall not be lynched. No matter what his crime, he is entitled to trial by law and a legal execution. The only exception is the Italian, who in this respect has been placed on terms of equality with the negro. If the Italian kills a white man, that is, a non Italian, he is likely to be lynched for it.

This rule has prevailed in all parts of the state. As long as the Italians in New Orleans confined their killings to their own race no special attention was paid to the matter. When, however, they killed an American, Chief of Police Hennessy, eleven were lynched. It should be said, by the way, that the excuse given by the Italians for the Hennessy assassination was that he interfered in an Italian quarrel. The Provenzanos and Matrangas had quarreled and declared a vendetta against each other. Hennessy, who was a friend of the Provenzanos, interfered, bringing himself, so the Italian assassins said, under the Italian vendetta code. It was the same in St. John the Baptist, where the killing of a creole by an Italian resulted in the lynching of all the Italians in the parish jail; while in Madison the mere assault on Dr. Hodge was considered good ground for wholesale lynching. Perhaps the situation there was simply given in the interviews with leading citizens of Madison, who declared that the hanging of the Italian prisoners was necessary in the interest of "white supremacy," the battle-cry of the North Louisiana Anglo-Saxons.

In the matter of law and order there has been a marked improvement among the Italians. If the Mafia ever existed, it is thoroughly dead now. It was believed in by the Italians themselves, and many of the better class paid blackmail to those who used the name of Mafia to frighten them with. The vendetta prevails among the newly arrived immigrants, but they soon drop it and go to law to settle their disputes. Formerly it was considered dishonorable and cowardly for a Sicilian to testify in a court against an oppressor; but now all do so. The amount of crime among them is small and decreasing. Their worst weakness is the hereditary tendency to take immediate vengeance for a wrong with the knife, pistol or the shotgun. In the second generation the Italian-American is an American, industrious, progressive and public-spirited.

Such is the race which now constitutes the largest foreign element in the population of Louisiana, and offers the state the best assurance that it will not become a second Africa, like the coast country of South Carolina. It has been difficult to get white immigrants to settle in the bottom lands of the Mississippi. Other foreigners will not come. They fear the heat and the malaria. The men from the North and West who have lately come into Louisiana have, without exception, settled in the pinelands or prairies. The white immigration into the rich alluvial lands of the Lafourche, Teche, Atchafalaya and Mississippi, the delta of the great river, has been nearly wholly Italian. It has fared well there and increased, and it is rapidly substituting white for negro labor, and accomplishing results that would have been impossible in any other way. In spite of the prejudices that exist, the mob outbreaks and the lynchings, the Italian is rapidly solving the negro problem in Louisiana. If the immigration from Italy keeps up, the Italian element will in time be preponderating in many parts of Louisiana. Outrages like that at Madison prove only a temporary check to this population movement. There are many who do not like the change from the old times and object to these modern Latins, but considering the rapidity with which the prejudice against them has weakened in the last few years, it is probable that it will have completely disappeared in another decade.

San Francisco Call
February 10, 1901

Grave but Uncorroborated Accusations are Made Against Chief Sullivan and Captain Wittman

Witnesses Repeat What Chinese Have Told Them of the Creation and Payment of Police Blackmail Fund to Insure Immunity

Legislative Investigators Receive Startling Testimony Which Proves That San Francisco is a Slave Market for Sale of Chinese Girls

The first week of the legislative inquiry into the alleged corruption of the Police Department is ended and still there is nothing more than hearsay testimony and suspicious collateral circumstances to prove that Chinese have bribed officials for immunity in gambling and social vice. At the sessions of the investigating committee yesterday witnesses testified that many years ago the Police Department was unquestionably corrupt in its relations with Chinese and that bribes were offered even to the chief of police

Testimony was given that Chinese gamblers have told white men that they paid blackmail to the Police Department, that Sergeant Brophy was the collector for the department and that Chief of Police Sullivan and Captain Wittman had given assurances that the police would not molest gamblers or disturb illegal houses if the money was paid.

This testimony is the most direct in its accusations of any which has been given during the investigation, but at best it is the testimony of Chinese presented through the medium of white go-betweens. The names of the Chinese who are said to have made these damaging assertions are known, and the coolies will probably be called by the committee.

In support of this testimony was evidence tending to show that gambling in Chinatown is now being conducted absolutely without check; that in the last few months the Chinese have been more daring and open in their operations and have conducted themselves as if they were assured of protection. A lawyer swore that the Chinese keepers of disreputable houses, which he was employed to protect, informed him that they had no further use for his services as they were dealing directly with the police. They told him that if he could assure them absolute immunity in gambling and social vice they would pay him thousands of dollars and would give many other thousands to persons who would fix the police.

It was also testified that even now announcements are posted on the walls of Chinatown giving information of the sale of slave girls in this city. That San Francisco is a slave market for Chinese girls was therefore for the first time announced in a judicial proceeding. These, in outline, were the developments yesterday in the inquiry.

The courtroom was crowded to the doors yesterday morning when the legislative investigators resumed their inquiry. The affair has been a subject of great public interest since its commencement and the developments of each day simply add to this interest. The poice placed a witness on the stand yesterday and had the chagrin of knowing that they had committed a most serious blunder. They called E.A. Finn, a watchman employed by the Chinese. He has worked in Chinatown for ten years and swore that he never saw to his own knowledge a house of bad repute or a gambling house in the district. That sort of testimony had the expected effect upon the committee. John Boyle, the Examiner reporter, told how he had secured for Assemblyman Wright the privilege of playing fantan.

Ex-Chief of Police Patrick Crowley was one of the most interesting witnesses of the day. His testimony left no doubt upon at least two points of the inquiry. He declared that it is extremely difficult and always has been for the Police Department to suppress gambling in the Chinese district. Further than that Chief Crowley said that there is no question that in times past there has been corruption in the Police Department in reference to Chinese. Not only was this the fact, but Chief Crowley declared that an effort was even made to bribe him.

His testimony consequently was of extreme interest. He said that the great obstacle to the suppression of gambling is the extreme difficulty under which the police must secure competent evidence. The Chinese use implements in their gambling which are apparently innocent. As far as Captain Wittman is concerned, Chief Crowley said that he had never found anything which convinced him of the dishonesty of that officer. When the charges were brought several years ago against Captain Wittman, ex-Chief Crowley said that he believed the charges to be true. Investigation convinced him, however, of his error.

As far as police corruption is concerned ex-Chief Crowley said that twenty years ago there was corruption in the department and twenty-three men were dismissed for dishonesty. What the character of the present administration may be the witness did not presume to say. About six years ago ex-Chief Crowley said that a deliberate effort was made to bribe him. He was offered $6000 if he would permit abandoned women to live on the first floors of houses. He, of course, declined to do so.

The next witness was the Rev. Dr. Gardner, who translated a notice which has been and is now posted on the walls of Chinatown. It is a notice and announcement of the sale of slave girls who are held in bondage in Sullivan alley. This is the first instance, perhaps, in this city in a judicial inquiry where the authoritative statement has been made that San Francisco is today a slave market. Not only this, but Dr. Gardner told of other signs which showed that in Chinatown today Chinese girls are for sale. This, in a way, is one of the most startling bits of testimony given at the investigation.

Dr. Gardner also testified that it is as easy to get into a Chinese gambling game as it is to enter a courtroom in the Hall of Justice. He has heard also that gambling in Chinatown appears to go on without interference through some arrangement with someone. The houses are being beautified and are being made alluring, and remarks have naturally followed this condition of affairs. As far as any direct allegations were concerned Dr. Gardner could make none. He showed, however, that crime and vice are rampant and are growing very rapidly.

Jerome Millard, an interpreter, gave the startling testimony that he was told by Chinese that they paid their corruption fund to Sergeant Brophy and were assured that if the money were paid Chief Sullivan and Captain Wittman would guarantee immunity.

Robert Ferral related his woes as an attorney who had lost employment by Chnese slave owners. He declared that his clients told him that they were dealing directly with the police. A recess was then taken until 9:30 o'clock tomorrow morning.

Grave but Uncorroborated Accusations

Tells of Slavery and Police Bribery

Yesterday's Session Produces Important Testimony From Men of Standing in Community

While yesterday's sessions of the legislative committee's investigation of the Police Department were devoid of any sensational features, the testimony was of a most important character.

That gambling and vice had joined hands to corrupt the Police Department was testified to by ex-Chief of Police Crowley, who not only had heard a few years ago that some of his officers were dishonest, but had been approached himself with the view of allowing the criminal element of Chinatown to be guaranteed immunity.

Another important fact was brought out, namely, that Chinese gamblers and lottery dealers had openly claimed that they had paid money to Chief Sullivan and Captain Wittman. The testimony was merely hearsay, but such as it was, it behooves the Chief and his captain to disprove it.

Flaring immorality and the barter for gold of human chattels were told of by Rev. Dr. John E. Gardner, who is, without doubt, the best qualified man in the United States to testify as to the doings of the Chinese in this city. For many years Dr. Gardner has waged war against the slave dealers in his capacity as Chinese inspector and interpreter for the federal government. His testimony yesterday might have referred to the city of Peking rather than to San Francisco, so terrible were the facts disclosed.

For the slave trade which exists in San Francisco the local police cannot be wholly blamed. Corrupt federal officials have been exposed many times, all of whom were in league with the slave dealers. For many years The Call waged war on the slave dealers and their white allies and today the bars are closely guarded by the government to prevent the importation of the female wares.

At the morning session of the legislative investigation yesterday, Speaker Pendleton of the Assembly and Arthur Fist, who fathered the "searchlight," were on hand to witness the proceedings. Although the session was called for 10 o'clock, there were no witnesses present until an hour later.

Reporting: Immigrants 1803-1931

Alden Boyle, a student of the high school, was the first witness called. He testified that he was a brother of J.J. Boyle, the reporter for the Examiner who had previously given evidence to the committee. The witness had accompanied his brother to Chinatown when the latter bought lottery tickets. He went to Chinatown six times and visited about twenty lottery rooms. Boyle saw his brother buy tickets and had himself purchased some. Many white men were in the lottery rooms. Witness had never visited a fantan game.

At the request of Attorney Dunne, who represents the police, D. A Finn, a watchman in Chinatown, was called to the witness stand. It would have been better if Finn had not been put forward, for he made a sorry exhibition of himself. In his efforts to prove that white men were not allowed to play fantan Finn went so far as to describe the Celestial quarter as being as pure as snow. He furnished considerable amusement to the members of the committee and the crowd of spectators.

Watchman Finn in a Forgetful Mood

He Is Placed on the Stand by the Police, But Makes a Very Poor Witness

Finn was examined by Assemblyman Webber, and in reply to questions said: "I am a watchman in Chinatown. I watch stores, loading-houses, family houses and warehouses. There are no gambling places in my district. There were a few fantan games some time ago, but none now. I don't know of any houses of ill-fame, or lottery places being in my district. I have never seen white men play fantan with Chinese. They will never let a white man in. Once I wanted to show some visitors how the game was played, and I asked the gamblers to let us come in. They let us in the room but there was no game in progress. I am not a special officer and have no star. I am well known to the Chinese. I know where 731 Pacific Street is. I have never been in it, but have seen white men go in." (This is the place where Witness Boyle purchased lottery tickets.) "The white men who went in were police officers. I never saw any other white men go in there. I have seen Chinese women in houses, but never saw anything to offend the eye."

"Do you know of any houses in Chinatown being used for immoral purposes?"

Grave but Uncorroborated Accusations

"I cannot say that I do."

"You watch all that property you have described and know for what use each house is put to, do you not?"

"Yes"

"Will you not swear that some of those houses were used for immoral purposes?"

"I will not swear that some of them were so used."

"You never saw a fantan game?"

"No, I have been in houses where I was told it was played, but never saw the game."

The witness then stated that opium was smoked in almost every house in Chantown, but that there were no places where men went to in order to smoke. At the request of Mr. Webber the witness described the buildings which are on either side of Baker alley.

"Is not Baker alley the most notorious in Chinatown?"

"No, there are no gambling dens there."

"Are there any houses of ill-fame there?"

"Women live there, but I cannot say they lead immoral lives."

"Do you mean to tell us that in your experience in Chinatown you do not know that these houses in Baker alley were houses of ill-fame and that the women who live there lead notoriously immoral lives?"

"Only what I have heard."

"Will you swear that white men don't play fantan, or cannot get into the gambling rooms where it is played?"

"I won't swear they don't play and I won't swear they can't get in."

"That will do"

Reporter J.J. Boyle was recalled and was asked for the address of the house where he went on Friday night with Assemblyman Wright, where the latter played fantan with Chinese. The witness stated that the house was at 808 Dupont Street, and the room they played in was on the second floor. He described the place as "a big Chinese restaurant." The witness denied making any previous arrangements for the game, but divulged that he had made arrangements with a white man to take Mr. Wright and the witness to the game. This admission caused a loud laugh in the courtroom, and Attorney Dunne asked that Boyle furnish the name of the white man with whom arrangements to visit the game had been made. Boyle promised to have the man on hand when wanted by the committee.

Ex-Chief P. Crowley on Witness Stand

Tells of His Experience with Chinese and Offers Made to Corrupt Him

The afternoon session commenced sharp on time and ex-Chief of Police Patrick Crowley was the first witness called. Chairman Knowland put the questions to the ex-Chief, who testified as follows:

"I have lived in the city for more than fifty years and was chief of police for twenty-five years. That was the only position I ever held in the department. I am now connected with the Hibernia Bank. I can say nothing as to the police methods of this city at the present time. I was sick when I left the department and have not taken any interest but in my own business."

"I want your opinion as an ex-chief of police of this city as to the best methods to suppress gambling in Chinatown."

"That is a hard job."

"Were you ever able to suppress it?"

"I did all I could."

"Why is it difficult to suppress fantan games and lottery?"

"It is difficult to secure the legal evidence."

"Do you think it is the fault of the laws?"

"To convict in these cases we must have certain testimony. The law might be amended to allow the introduction of certain evidence. The Chinese use beans, peas, buttons and even candy in playing fantan. The law ought to allow these things to be introduced as evidence in gambling cases. Regarding immorality in Chinatown, I used my efforts to have a law passed which allowed the reputation of a house to be introduced in evidence. To suppress immorality the only way to do is to blockade the water where the houses are. It would take 200 men to do this in Chinatown. I have done it, but it left the rest of the city without protection. I know of the slave trade existing in the city. It exists far differently to what most people think. Some newspapermen understand the methods of the dealers because they have investigated the subject."

The ex-chief then went into detail as to how the slave dealers get hold of young women of their race and force them to lead lives of shame. He told how women are brought from China, and under the guise of being

Grave but Uncorroborated Accusations

native-born Americans, married if necessary to a Chinaman to satisfy the courts, and then placed in the slave dens. He also told how respectable women are torn from their husbands or families by the slave dealers using American courts of law.

"A trumped-up charge of larceny is made, warrants are issued, the woman is arrested and taken away from the place where she lives into another city. There bail is furnished for her by one of the gang, the dealers get possession of her and that is the last seen of her by her friends. She is to be found in the slave dens of Chinatown."

Crowley Thinks That Wittman is Honest

Personally Questioned People Who Brought Charges Against the Captain

"What is your opinion of Captain Wittman's record in Chinatown?"

"I think he did his duty. Charges were made against him some years ago. I investigated them, personally questioned women and assured them of the protection of the law if they testified, and was satisfied that there was nothing in the charges against Wittman. He was acquitted by the police commissioners. No special complaint was ever made against Wittman from Chinatown. There is always trouble up there, however."

"Do you know of police corruption by the Chinese?"

"I have no personal knowledge, but heard rumors. Some years ago I discharged a number of officers who had done duty in Chinatown. No direct proof of corruption was forthcoming, but the conduct of the officers warranted dismissal."

"Was any offer ever made to you by the Chinese of a large sum of money in order that they might be allowed to gamble and run houses of ill fame?"

"Twenty years ago such an offer was made to me by the gamblers through an attorney who is now dead. Seven years ago an offer was made to me by the Chinese through a white man who had business dealings with them."

"What was that offer?"

"They wanted to be allowed to run houses of ill-fame unmolested by the police and offered me $6000. I had previously made the women move from the street floor to the floor upstairs and they wanted to be allowed to occupy their old quarters."

"Who was the white man who made this offer to you?"

"I prefer not to say. He is alive, but has no further dealings with the Chinese. He did not tell me the names of the Chinese who had asked him to make me that offer. I know that he told them that it was useless to see me and that all the gold in the world would not make me flinch from my duty. They insisted, however, that he come to me with the offer. I never heard a complaint of police blackmail. I never knew of white men visiting Chinese houses of ill-fame except through rumor."

Tells of Traffic in Slave Girls

Rev. Dr. Gardner Throws Light on Chinese Bartering Girls in This City

Rev. John E. Gardner was then called to the witness stand and examined by Assemblyman Schillig. The witness testified as follows:

"I am an inspector of Chinese and interpreter for the federal government and engaged in carrying out the provisions of the Chinese exclusion laws. I speak Chinese and studied it in China, Australia, Canada and in this country. I am constantly in Chinatown. I have never seen white men play fantan, but I have seen them go into places where signs were displayed that the game was played there. I have never been in the lottery places. They also have signs displayed. My work in Chinatown and elsewhere is to prevent the illegal landing of Chinese and not to suppress vice. I saw some of the gambling and lottery signs last night in Chinatown. The signs showed that fantan, pi-gow and lottery games were carried on inside."

The witness was here handed a red paper bearing Chinese characters and was asked if he had ever seen a sign like it displayed in front o a gambling place. He answered in the negative.

"The gambling house signs are mostly written on white paper. I have seen signs like this posted on the street corners. I was in Chinatown when a reporter asked me to translate this sign. I did so and he tore it down. It was posted up on the corner of Sacramento and Dupont streets on the southwest side."

"Will you translate that writing for us?"

Grave but Uncorroborated Accusations

"I will give you a free translation. It reads as follows: 'The stock in trade and good will of a house of prostitution for sale. Madame Law Wong Sut of this city secretly escaped and returned to China on the 14th day of the present month, leaving behind the business, stock and trade of the house of prostitution on Sullivan Alley. Madame Law Wong Sut owed a lot of money on goods advanced to her by people of wealth. The creditors have agreed to take the whole business and sell it to pay her debts. Any countryman wishing the business, let him go to the house of prostitution and talk to the creditors. As to the amounts owed by Madame Law Wong Sut they will be reported by the 20th of the month. Bills will be presented up to that time and not after. This notice is given so that there may be no after talk. Dated Qwong Suey, 26th year, 14th day, last month.'"

"That date corresponds with February 4, 1901."

"Do you know where that house is?"

"I do not. It is an easy matter to recognize the Chinese houses of ill-fame. They all have lattice work windows, look-out windows and painted women behind the windows soliciting men who pass along the street. These houses exist in Sullivan and Ross alleys."

"Have you seen white men go into these places or young white men?"

"Yes, I have seen these women soliciting soldiers, mostly young soldiers. I have never seen white boys go into these houses."

"Have you seen white men and boys go into the lottery places?"

"I have seen men and young men go into them. They went in a few at a time. I cannot say that I saw police officers near when these men went in."

"Are there more lotteries and gambling places in the last few months than previously?"

"I am afraid to say I have noticed that."

"Have you heard the Chinese talking about immunity from arrest?"

A Tranquil Air Pervades Chinatown

"I have not heard them so talking, but there was a feeling in the air that something of the kind existed. As the Chinese say, there was a tranquil air. The number of lights in front of the gambling and lottery places were increased and the Chinese would go in and out of these places in a free manner, not at all alarmed or careful".

"What do you know of the slave trade?"

"As a federal officer I am most familiar with it. I have prevented the landing of many girls destined for the slave dens. I have rescued many girls from the dens while aiding the ladies of the missions."

"Do you know of girls being sold in Chinatown."

"I do. I have one in my charge now who was recently rescued from a house of ill-fame by the mission people. The girl is a minor. She will be deported to China by order of the federal courts. Girls rescued from the slave dens have told me in the mission homes the prices they were sold for. They all tell the same unhappy story. Many have been lured from their homes and forced to lead lives of shame by their owners. They are brutally treated and intimidated. I have often seen signs displayed announcing girls for sale. There is not the slightest doubt in my mind that the sign I have translated is a sign announcing the sale of human beings. I recently translated similar signs for Captain Wittman."

"Have the lookouts for the gambling places been as active in the past few months as they were previously?"

"No, they have not, but the solicitors for the lottery places have been most active. They accost people passing along and say to them, 'Tickets, gentlemen, tickets, gentlemen.' It is as easy to go into one of those lottery places as it is to come into this courtroom."

"What remarks have you heard the Chinese make as to the air of tranquility you have spoken of?"

"I have heard them say the tranquil state was not secured for nothing. The gamblers seem to be having a good time. the lookouts have been withdrawn and the places seem to run without interference."

"Knowing the Chinese as you do, what would you infer from the remarks you heard that the tranquil time was not secured for nothing?"

"I inferred that gambling was to be allowed to go unmolested."

"Have you ever complained to the police of the conditions of Chinatown?"

"I have. Captain Wittman helped to close up the highbinders. If that work had been kept up they would all have been driven out of the city. Today they are very much alive."

"How do you know that?"

Grave but Uncorroborated Accusations

"On account of the frequent murders in Chinatown. I have seen Chinese men accost white men and ask them to go in to the houses of ill fame."

Accusing Testimony Against the Police

*Interpreter Millard Says Chinese
Spoke of Bribing Chief Sullivan and Wittman*

Jerome Millard was then called and testified that he was a Chinese interpreter to the courts of this city and county. He had acted as interpreter for twenty years. He was in Chinatown every day. He talked freely with Chinese and mingled with them.

"I know," said the witness, "all the gamblers by sight. I have known Qwong Hing, Chan Chin, San Jose Charlie, Buckeye and Wong Fook for many years. They are all interested in gambling houses. I have talked with Qwong Hing about police protection. He acknowledged to me that gamblers were to pay for police protection. He asked me how the white people felt about Chinese gambling and running houses of ill fame. I cannot remember all the conversation I had with the men mentioned. This occurred three years ago. They told me they belonged to a committee to secure police protection for the gamblers and keepers of the dens. Qwong Hing told me that the future management of the gambling houses would be in the hands of Chief Sullivan and Captain Wittman. This was three weeks ago. I have talked with them about a corruption fund. They said they had to pay the police for the privilege of gambling. They spoke of Sergeant Brophy as the man who collected the money once a week."

"For what purpose did they say they gave the money to the police?"

"To secure immunity from arrest."

"Who told you this?"

"Quon Been and another man whose name I cannot remember. They said they gave the money to Brophy once a week. They said the rate paid was $10 for a gambling house and lotteries. They told me that certain of the police had made promises of protection."

"Whom did they mention?"

"Chief Sullivan and Captain Wittman."

"Did they state that they had received personal assurance from the chief and from Captain Wittman of immunity from arrest?"

"That was the idea I got from them."

In reply to a question from Attorney Dunne the witness admitted that he was friendly to the Examiner and was friendly with Reporter Boyle. The witness had accompanied Boyle through Chinatown on many occasions.

Chinese Discharge Attorney Ferral

Judge Robert Ferral then took the stand and testified that he had for many years been employed by the Chinese. He formerly had a contract with them.

"What was the nature of your duties?"

"I represented the women of ill-repute when they were arrested."

"Do you still represent them?"

"No, I do not. A few weeks ago they told me indirectly they had no further use for an attorney as they were doing business with the police direct."

"The fees you got went to the police?"

"I suppose so."

Judge Ferral, who was in a convivial mood, volunteered a statement when he was excused from the witness stand. He said that the Chinese gamblers had asked him if he could fix things with the police so that they might carry on gambling and maintain the dens without fear of arrest.

"They said that there would be thousands of dollars in it for me if I could fix it and thousands for the police. I consulted Attorney Dunne, but, of course, we could not do it. We had no power with the Police Commission to alter the law. I told the Chinese it was impossible, but that 'Barkis was willing.'"

Whether Judge Ferral made his last statement in jest or in earnest was not asked by the committee of inquiry, but it is possible that he may be called upon to explain what he meant.

The inquiry will be resumed tomorrow morning and the committee will sit morning, noon and night until all the evidence is in.

Strong Speeches to the Delegates

Big Raid is Made on Chinese Gaming Club

Ninety-Five Fantan Players Captured by Captain Wittman and Squad of Police

One of the largest raids that has occurred in Chinatown for some time was made last night by Captain Wittman and a squad of police. The gambling club of Qwong Hing at the corner of Clay Street and Waverly Place was broken into and ninety-five fantan players captured. All were booked at the Hall of Justice. With the exception of a number of Japanese all were immediately released on bail.

The capture was a clever one. A drainage pipe leading from the gaming room was located several days ago and plans for a grand haul were immediately laid. Sergeant Donovan, followed by a number of patrolmen in citizens' clothes, approached the place, and when they commenced to chop the barred doors down the keeper of the game attempted to dispose of the paraphernalia by dumping it down the pipe to the sewer.

Sergeant Christiansen had removed a section of the sewer pipe, and when the evidence came down he caught it in a basket. The players were then placed under arrest.

San Francisco Call
November 23, 1901

Strong Speeches to the Delegates

Sentiments Favoring Protection to American Labor Are Wildly Cheered.

The Chinese Exclusion Convention completed its labors yesterday after the adoption of one of the most important as well as vigorous memorials on the Chinese question ever addressed to the President and Congress of the United States. The attitude of the people of California and of the entire Pacific Coast toward the problem of unrestricted immigration of Asiatics to these shores as represented in the convention was distinctly outlined, and its language cannot fail to be understood in the East as being the spontaneous outburst of a united people against the imposition upon them of a grievous wrong.

The delegates gathered in force yesterday morning and listened with enthusiasm to many speakers. Only one theme was discussed, only one idea advanced, namely, unalterable resistance to the project of unrestricted Chinese immigration to America. The danger of a Mongolian invasion in the event of the refusal of Congress to re-enact the exclusion law was pointed out in forceful language by all the speakers. The delegates cheered heartily at every patriotic sentiment voiced by the orators, and particularly when the necessity of protecting American labor against foreign competition was urged. The members of the convention showed by their zeal that they were in accord with the speakers.

The report of the committee on permanent organization was the first matter to engage the attention of the delegates at the morning session. The recommendation that the temporary officers be made permanent was adopted amid cheers. It was expected that the memorial committee would be able to file its report, but the announcement by Chairman Geary that further time was required by the committee resulted in the desired action being taken. There being no definite business before the convention, speechmaking was indulged in. Assistant United States District Attorney Duncan E. McKinlay was introduced by the chair, and that gentleman delivered an able address in which he reviewed the Chinese question from the standpoint of the District Attorney's office. The legal aspects of the issue were capably presented, the speaker's remarks at times evoking hearty applause. So favorably did he impress his hearers that at the close of his speech he was honored by a vote of thanks for his brilliant oratorical effort.

The Rev. Dr. William Rader followed with a witty address, in which he reviewed the Chinese question from the standpoint of morality and religion. His allusions to the vices prevailing in San Francisco's Chinatown, and of their effect upon the whole community, were impressively advanced, and his remark that the proper place in which to Christianize the Chinese was in China and not in this country, evoked cheers. The address was replete with statistical information, and it was listened to with profound interest by all present.

Congressman Woods carried away the banner by a characteristic speech in which he informed the convention "that with its assistance all h—l couldn't beat the exclusion law." Woods was in deep earnest, and all his utterances were accompanied by vigorous gestures and a beating of the rostrum with a vigor that threatened to convert it into kindling wood. He assured the convention that the California delegation in Congress would never give up the exclusion fight, and when he sought to close what he termed his "razzle-dazzle" address, the crowd yelled lustily for more. Woods obliged the delegates further, and when he concluded the delegates gave him three hearty cheers.

The closing address of the morning session was by Mayor Snyder of Los Angeles. During the afternoon the representatives of various labor organizations delivered brief addresses. Dr. Williamson, president of the Board of Health, talked of the Chinese curse in San Francisco and frequently evoked applause. Mr. Taylor of the State Grange spoke in behalf of the farmers of California, and in a logical speech showed the evil effects unrestricted immigration of Chinese to California would exert upon rural pursuits in this state.

The main event of the afternoon session was the reading and adoption of the memorial to President Roosevelt and to Congress. Prior to the filing of the report of the committee Supervisor Reed's motion that a committee be appointed to wait upon Rev. Father Peter C. Yorke with the request that he address the convention was carried, and Reed was detailed for the task. A motion to adjourn just before Rev. Mr. Yorke's arrival was voted down, and when the clergyman appeared he was warmly greeted. He spoke at some length, and at the conclusion of his speech several motions of more or less importance were made and carried. The convention then adjourned *sine die.*

San Francisco Call
November 23, 1901

Memorial of the Exclusion Convention
Addressed to the President and Congress

To the President and the Congress of the United States: Pursuant to a call officially issued by the city of San Francisco, there assembled in that city on the 21st day of November, 1901, for the purpose of expressing the sentiments of the State of California, a convention composed of representatives of county supervisors, city councils, trade, commercial and civic organizations to the number of three thousand, and without dissent it was resolved to memorialize the president and the Congress of the United States as follows:

Soon after the negotiation of the Burlingame treaty in 1868 large numbers of Chinese coolies were brought to this country under contract. Their numbers so increased that in 1878 the people of the state made a practically unanimous demand for the restriction of the immigration. Our white population suffered in every department of labor and trade, having in numerous instances been driven out of employment by the competition of the Chinese. The progress of the state was arrested because so long as the field was occupied by Chinese a new and desirable immigration was impossible. After a bitter struggle remedial legislation was passed in 1882 and was renewed in 1892, to run for a period of ten years. Your memorialists, in view of the fact that the present so-called Geary law expires by limitation on May 5 next, and learning that you have been petitioned against its re-enactment, believe that it is necessary for them to repeat and to reaffirm the reasons which, in their judgment, require the re-enactment and the continued enforcement of the law.

The effects of Chinese exclusion have been most advantageous to the state. The 75,000 Chinese residents of California in 1880 have been reduced, according to the last census, to 45,600; and whereas, the white settlement of California by Caucasians had been arrested prior to the adoption of these laws, a healthy growth of the state in population has marked the progress of recent years. Every material interest of the state has advanced and prosperity has been our portion. Were the restriction laws relaxed we are convinced that our working population would be displaced, and the noble structure of our state, the creation of American ideas and industry would be imperiled if not destroyed. The lapse of time has only confirmed your memorialists in their conviction, from their knowledge derived from actually coming in contact with the Chinese, that they are a non-assimilative race and by every standard of American thought undesirable as citizens. Although they have been frequently employed and treated with decent consideration ever since the enactment of the exclusion law in 1882, which was the culmination and satisfaction of California's patriotic purpose, they have not in any sense altered their racial characteristics and have not socially or otherwise assimilated with our people. To quote the Imperial Chinese Consul General in San Francisco: "They work more cheaply than whites; they live more cheaply; they send their money out of the country to China; most of them have no intention of remaining in the United States, and they do not adopt American manners, but live in colonies and not after the American fashion."

Physical Assimilation Impossible

Until this year no statute had been passed by the state forbidding their intermarriage with the whites, and yet during their long residence but few intermarriages have taken place and the offspring has been invariably degenerate. It is well established that the issue of the Caucasian and the Mongolian does not possess the virtue of either, but develops the vices of both. So physical assimilation is out of the question.

It is well known that the vast majority of Chinese do not bring their wives with them in their immigration because of their purpose to return to their native land when a competency is earned. Their practical status among us has been that of single men competing at low wages against not only men of our own race, but men who have been brought up by our civilization to family life and civic duty. They pay little taxes, they support no institutions—neither school, church nor theater; they remain steadfastly, after all these years, a permanently foreign element. The purpose, no doubt, for enacting the exclusion laws for periods of ten years is due to the intention of Congress of observing the progress of these people under American institutions, and now it has been clearly demonstrated that they cannot, for the deep and ineradicable reasons of race and mental organization, assimilate with our own people and be molded as are other races into strong and composite American stock.

We respectfully represent that their presence excludes a desirable population and that there is no necessity whatever for their immigration. The immigration laws of this country now exclude pauper and contract labor from every land. All Chinese immigration of the coolie class is both pauper and contract labor. It is not a voluntary immigration. The Chinese Six Companies of California deal in Chinese labor as a commodity. Prior to the exclusion they freely imported coolies, provided for them, farmed out their services and returned them, and if they should die their bones, pursuant to a superstitious belief, to their native land.

America is the asylum for the oppressed and liberty-loving people of the world, and the implied condition of their admission to this country is allegiance to its government and devotion to its institutions. It is hardly necessary to say that the Chinese are not even bona fide settlers, as the Imperial Chinese Consul General admits.

We respectfully represent that American labor should not be exposed to the destructive competition of aliens who do not, will not and cannot take up the burdens of American citizenship, whose presence is an economic blight and a patriotic danger. It has been urged that the Chinese are unskilled and that they create wealth in field, mine and forest, which ultimately redounds to the benefit of the white skilled workingman. The Chinese are skilled and are capable of almost any skilled employment. They have invaded the cigar, shoe, broom, chemical, clothing, fruit canning, matchmaking and woolen manufacturing industries, and have displaced more than 4000 white men in these several employments in the city of San Francisco. As common laborers they have throughout California displaced tens of thousands of men. But this country is not solely concerned even in a coldly economic sense with the production of wealth.

Grave Danger of Over-Production

The United States has now a greater per capita of working energy than any other land. If it is stimulated by a non-assimilative and non-consuming race there is grave danger of overproduction and stagnation. The home market should grow with the population. But the Chinese, living on the most meager food, having no families to support, inured to deprivation, and hoarding their wages for use in their native land, whither they invariably return, cannot in any sense be regarded as consumers. Their earnings do not circulate nor are they reinvested—contrary to those economic laws which make for the prosperity of nations. For their services they may be said to be paid twice—first by their employer and then by the community. If we must have protection, is it not far better for us to protect ourselves against the man than against his trade? Our opponents maintain that the admission of the Chinese would cause an enlargement of our national wealth and a great increase of production, but the distribution of wealth and not its production is today our most serious public question. In this age of science and invention the production of wealth can well be left to take care of itself. It is its equitable distribution that must now be the concern of the country.

The increasing recurrence of strikes in modern times must have convinced everyone that their recent settlement is nothing more than a truce. It is not a permanent industrial peace. The new organization of capital and labor that is now necessary to bring about lasting peace and harmony between those engaged in production will require greater sympathy, greater trust and confidence and a clearer mutual understanding between the employers and the employed. Any such new organization will require a closer union to be formed between them. These requirements can never be fulfilled between the individuals of races so alien to one another as ourselves and the Chinese.

The Chinese are only capable of working under the present unsatisfactory system. All progress then to an improved organization of capital and labor would be arrested. We might have greater growth, but never greater development. It was estimated by the commissioner of labor that there were a million idle men in the United States in 1886. Certainly the 76,000 Chinese in California at that time stood for 76,000 white men waiting for employment, and the further influx of Chinese in any considerable numbers would precipitate the same condition again, if not indeed make it chronic. If the United States increases in population at the rate of 12 per cent per decade it will have nearly 230,000,000 people in 100 years. Our inventive genius and the constant improvements being made in machinery will greatly increase our per capita productive capacity. If it be our only aim to increase our wealth so as to hold our own in the markets of the world are we not, without the aid of Chinese coolies, capable of doing it and at the same time preserving the character of our population and insuring the perpetuity of our institutions? It is not wealth at any cost that sound public policy requires, but that the country be developed with equal pace and with a desirable population which stands not only for industry but for citizenship.

Reporting: Immigrants 1803-1931

Chinese Crowding Out Americans

In their appeal to the cupidity of farmers and orchardists the proponents of Chinese immigration have stated that the Chinese are only common laborers, and by this kind of argument they have attempted to disarm the skilled labor organizations of the country; but we have shown you that the Chinese are skilled and are capable of becoming skilled. As agriculturists they have crowded out the native population and driven the country boy from the farm to the city, where he meets their skilled competition in many branches of industry. But shall husbandry be abandoned to a servile class? Shall the boys and girls of the fields and of the orchards be deprived of their legitimate work in the harvest? Shall not our farmers be encouraged to look to their own households and to their own neighbors for labor? Shall the easy methods of contract employment be encouraged? We are warned by history that the free population of Rome was driven by slave labor from the country into the city, where it became a mob and a rabble, ultimately compassing the downfall of the republic. The small farms were destroyed, and under an overseer large farms were cultivated, which led Pliny to remark that "great estates ruined Italy."

The experience of the South with slave labor warns us against unlimited Chinese immigration, considered both as a race question and as an economic problem. The Chinese, if permitted to freely enter this country, would create race antagonisms which would ultimately result in great public disturbance. The Caucasian will not tolerate the Mongolian. As ultimately all government is based on physical force, the white population of this country will not without resistance suffer itself to be destroyed. Economically it was thought wise at one time to employ negro slaves, but the accumulated wealth of the South was wiped out by an appalling expenditure of blood and money, precipitating conditions which bore with terrible force upon a people which were once considered great and prosperous. The cornerstone of their structure was slavery, and the cornerstone of any structure based upon the employment of Chinese coolies is servile labor. It is repugnant to our form of society and to our ideas of government to segregate a labor class and regard it only as its capacity for work. If we were to return to the ante-bellum ideas of the South, now happily discarded, the Chinese would satisfy every requirement of a slave or servile class. They work incessantly, they are docile and they would not be concerned about

Memorial of the Exclusion Convention

their political conditions, but such suggestions are repulsive to American civilization. America has dignified work and made it honorable. Manhood gives title to rights, and the government being ruled by majorities is largely controlled by the very class which servile labor would supersede, namely, the free and independent workingmen of America. The political power invested in men by this government shows the absolute necessity of keeping up the standard of population and not permitting it to deteriorate by contact with inferior and non-assimilative races.

Question Involves Our Civilization

But this is not alone a race, labor and political question. It is one which involves our civilization, and that interests the people of the world. The benefactors, scholars, soldiers and statesmen—the patriots and martyrs of mankind—have built our modern fabric firmly upon the foundation of religion, law, science and art. It has been rescued from barbarism and protected against the incursions of barbarians. Civilization in Europe has been frequently attacked and imperiled by the barbaric hordes of Asia. If the little band of Greeks at Marathon had not beaten back ten times their number of Asiatic invaders it is impossible to estimate the loss to civilization that would have ensued. When we contemplate what modern civilization owes to the two centuries of Athenian life, from which we first learned our lessons of civil and intellectual freedom, we can see how necessary it was to keep the Asiatic from breaking into Europe. Attila and his Asiatic hordes threatened Central Europe when the Gauls made their successful stand against them. The wave of Asiatic barbarism rolled back and civilization was again saved. The repulse of the Turks, who are of the Mongolian race, before Vienna finally made our civilization strong enough to take care of itself, and the danger of extinction by a military invasion from Asia passed away. We can meet and defend ourselves against an open foe, but an insidious foe under our generous laws would be in possession of the citadel before we are aware. The free immigration of Chinese would be for all purposes an invasion by Asiatic barbarians, against whom civilization in Europe has been frequently defended, fortunately for us. It is our inheritance to keep it pure and uncontaminated, as it is our purpose and destiny to broaden and enlarge it. We are trustees for mankind.

Reporting: Immigrants 1803-1931

In an age when the brotherhood of man has become more fully recognized we are not prepared to overlook the welfare of the Chinaman himself. We need have nothing on our national conscience because the Chinaman has a great industrial destiny in his own country. Few realize that China is yet a sparsely populated country. Let their merchants, travelers and students then come here as before to carry back to China the benefits of our improvements and experiments. Let American ideas of progress and enterprise be planted on Chinese soil. Our commerce with China since 1880 has increased more than 50 per cent. Our consular service reports that "the United States is second only to Great Britain in goods sold to the Chinese. The United States buys more goods from China than does any other nation, and her total trade with China, exports and imports, equals that of Great Britain, not including the colonies, and is far ahead of that of any other country."

Commerce is not sentimental and has not been affected by our policy of exclusion. The Chinese government, knowing the necessities of the situation, being familiar with the fact that almost every country has imposed restrictions upon the immigration of Chinese coolies, does not regard our attitude as an unfriendly act. Indeed, our legislation has been confirmed by treaty. Nor are the Chinese unappreciative of the friendship of the United States recently displayed in saving possibly the empire itself from dismemberment. So, therefore, America is at no disadvantage in its commercial dealings with China on account of the domestic policy of Chinese exclusion.

Therefore every consideration of public duty, the nation's safety and the people's rights, the preservation of our civilization and the perpetuity of our institutions impel your memorialists to ask for the re-enactment of the exclusion laws which have for twenty years protected us against the gravest dangers, and which, were they relaxed, would imperil every interest which the American people hold sacred for themselves and their posterity.

New York Tribune
July 12, 1903

Some of the Peculiarities, Both Picturesque and Otherwise, Of Our Italian Fellow Citizens

From Sunny Italy

Immigrants Bring Their Saints' Days With Them and Celebrate

Scattered about the walls of the smoking room of the new lodging house for newly arrived immigrants, which the Italian Benevolent Society has just opened in West Houston Street, a few doors beyond Macdougal Street, are frames containing specimens of paper money some forty-odd years ago by the Confederate States of America. The inscription upon the card to which the bills are fastened begins "Importanza." Then it proceeds to announce to the new arrival that the war is over.

There is no more apt illustration of the character of the swarthy men and women who for six or seven years now have been pouring in from the impoverished provinces of Italy. Most of them are the personification of guilelessness, and Confederate money is a rock that has wrecked many an Italian family bark before it was fairly out of the steerage.

Never before have the Italians of standing in this city taken such an interest in their incoming countrymen. There are many rich men in the various Italian colonies of Manhattan and Brooklyn, merchants, contractors, bankers and small manufacturers. They are contributing liberally to the support of the societies which look after immigrants.

The Society for the Protection of Italian Immigrants has its headquarters in Pearl Street, near the Battery, and is doing a great work keeping new arrivals out of the hands of the runners for the padrone boardinghouse keepers. These runners are themselves Italians, as likely as not from the same province as the immigrant, and would have a free hand with them if it was not for the interference of the society's agents.

The waiting room of the society's headquarters is a most interesting place. Sitting around on benches the other afternoon were three young

Italians from cities near Naples. At their sides or under their feet were the bags which contained their earthly possessions, which they guarded with the utmost care. They had been swaggering young bloods, perhaps, in their native Maddaloni or Marigliano—the rings in their ears, the brilliancy of their scarfs and the beads about their necks told that. But here in New York the swagger oozed out through the heels of their odd boots. They were mute, and shrank with apprehension with the noise of every truck that jolted over the Pearl Street cobbles. From the lapel of each dangled a ticket on which his destination up-state was plainly written. They fingered these from time to time, making sure that they were still in place—the only tangible thing to which they could cling.

The new lodging house, the one with the Confederate bill wall decoration, is as practical an Italian charity as could be devised. A large tenement has been taken and fitted up for one hundred men and women. In the basement are the smoking and baggage rooms. On the first floor are the dining room, kitchen and offices. Above are many dormitories and single rooms for families of immigrants who can afford to pay for extra services. The bedding on the low iron cots is spotless and everything about the place is as clean as a pin.

There were twenty immigrants in the lodgings when a Tribune reporter visited it. They had been in the country several days, and already they were beginning to take notice. They were waiting for friends to come for them or for employment at their various trades. Meantime they smoked long, black cheroots or short pipes, chatted quietly among themselves and looked out on the busy life of the street. In six months they will be speaking English after a fashion, and in a year or two they will have saved enough to send for their families or sweethearts. As soon as the legal time limit is passed they will take out their first papers and eventually become American voters—trust the Italian politician for that.

The contractors in the subway, in which many Italians are employed, had a chance a few weeks ago to learn how quickly the Italian laborer, the lowest class of immigrant, grasps American institutions. This particular institution was the strike, and the foreigners took to it as the babies of Mulberry Bend take to garlic and macaroni. Of course they had Irish walking delegates to start them, but it was not long until they outdid their teachers.

Some of the Peculiarities of our Italian Fellow Citizens

The walking delegates settled the strike to their satisfaction and personal profit. "You can go back to work," they said to the Italians.

"Doa we getta de hours?" demanded the spokesman of one gang.

"We getta de morea pay?" inquired the head of another party, those who had gone out for an increase in wages.

"You go back to work," ordered the walking delegate. "Same hours; same pay. We lost the strike."

The Italians were not so sure about that. They were filled with the strike idea and they refused to dig until they got what they wanted. Other workmen were put on the job, but not for long. The Italians knew the answer. They dropped rocks into the excavations. Their wives and children easily worked themselves into a frenzy, and the substitutes fled under a storm of sticks and stones. Eventually the Italians were re-employed, and in several instances they gained their demands.

Settlement workers say that the iniquitous padrone system is disappearing in this city. Railroad contractors, who can herd their men together and keep them in gangs, are still able to work the ignorant Italian, giving him little more than enough to keep body and soul together. In the city, however, where the laborers live in separate tenements, they cannot long be buncoed, and soon secure fair wages.

There is one thing in which the Italian never wavers, no matter how great a change in his station immigration may effect. He holds by his church and clings to all the religious festivals of his native town and province. If he does not know where the next meal is coming from he has a few pennies to buy candles for the patron saint of the Italian village which gave him birth. A mother's children may be crying for bread, but until the fire escape is decorated for the festival they cry in vain. Little children patter bare-footed through the rain to place their offering on a bedraggled street shrine, and never think of spending the pennies for gummy Italian toffy with which the venders try to tempt them.

"I have been working in this district for two years now," said a young woman connected with the West Side branch of the University Settlement, "and I've made a study of Italian celebrations, but I cannot tell where one leaves off and another begins."

This is due to the fact that people from widely separated parts of Italy are gathered together in the same district. There are almost as many saints as there are days in the year and someone is always celebrating.

Then there are general festivals to the celebration of which Italians come from all parts of the city.

The Ascension of Our Lady of Mount Carmel, one of the biggest of the annual festivals, will begin on July 16 and last the remainder of the week. It is celebrated in "Little Italy," one of the three big Italian colonies in Manhattan, because the Church of Our Lady of Mount Carmel is within its bounds, in East 115th Street, between First and Pleasant Aves. Italians from all parts of the city will march into "Little Italy" on the big days of the festival, headed by their bands and marching societies, all gayly caparisoned. Hundreds will come in from nearby towns the day before the festival begins, and remain several days afterward.

Tomorrow "Little Italy" will begin to decorate and otherwise prepare to do the Lady of Mount Carmel more honor than has ever come to her before in New York. Altars will be erected in several places. East 112th and neighboring streets will be spanned with row after row of small cups of colored glass. Filled with olive oil and provided with wicks, these "night lights" will glow for hours and add much to the beauty of the celebration. There is further illumination on the tenement house fronts, hand-painted transparencies, candles and oil caps being freely used. Italian and American flags fly from every possible point of vantage, and there is much green bunting in evidence.

The street altars are perhaps the most striking feature of the festival. They are built on the sidewalk, usually where two big tenements meet, and rise forty or fifty feet. Generally they are of wood, enameled or covered with bunting, with some attempt at fancy carving. The top pieces are most elaborate and follow various designs, generally allowing for floral decoration. Within the shrine are relief figures of the saints to be honored, and in front art; shelves for the candles of those who seek her favor. It is a poor shrine, indeed, that does not cost $1,000, and sometimes they are much more expensive. Shrines are erected in many of the tenement house windows. These are more simple, but an extravagance nevertheless, when one considers the means of those who erect them. The centre piece of the private shrines is a plaster figure of the patron saint. At night this is surrounded by candles. Poorer families have to be content with a cheap transparency of the saint illuminated with a single candle.

Marching in procession through the uptown streets will begin early next Thursday morning. The curbs, the stoops and the lower landings of the fire escapes will be packed with happy people, dressed in their best and brightest clothes. Marching clubs of one sort and another, with banners flying and their brass bands making no end of noise, will lead the way. As they pass the heads of the families which crowd the sidelines will halt their favorite society long enough to pin a few dollars in paper money to the society's banner. Before the marchers have completed the round of the quarter the banners of popular societies are almost hidden behind these gifts. The money is used to defray the expenses of the celebration.

There are many women and children in the procession—pretty, dark eyed girls in white dresses, and, if they are doing a particular penance, in bare feet perhaps; expansive matrons, with infants snuggled in their arms, trudging along with the rest, and on every face a smile. In the right parades the women carry lighted candles in their hands, and some have specially constructed headpieces bearing anywhere from a dozen to fifty lighted candles. The morning procession ends at the church in 115th Street, where there is a statue of Our Lady of Mount Carmel. This shrine is decorated with jewel offerings to the extent of thousands of dollars. Rings, with flashing diamonds, gold watches, earrings, chairs and bracelets are given up freely under the spell of excitement which the festival casts.

Nearly every one brings candles for the priests to burn in her honor. Some of these candles are ten feet in height and so heavy that it takes two men to carry them. The more expensive ones are hand painted or carved with figures of religious subjects. Decorated candles cost from $5 to $400, the belief being that the more expensive the candle, the greater favor will the saint return. During a celebration like this several tons of candles will be left behind after the services.

No one has yet appeared with energy enough to figure out the annual cost of the religious festivals of the Italian quarters. Some families have to save the year round in order to make a satisfactory showing at festival time, and do sufficient honor to the saint who has their destinies in hand. Were it not for their extravagance at festival time, and the hundreds of dollars of unnecessary expenditure for funerals, there would be vastly less suffering in the quarters. It is doubtful, however, if the people would be any happier. Deprive an Italian of a chance to honor his particular saint, or force him to bury a dead child without a procession of a dozen carriages, a brass band and no end of floral pieces, and life is a miserable and worthless thing indeed to him.

Reporting: Immigrants 1803-1931

Of the three distinctive Italian quarters in Manhattan—"Little Italy," "Mulberry Bend" and "Richmond Hill"— the last, which is the newest, is perhaps the most interesting. One may be taking liberties in calling this new district "Richmond Hill," but that is the historical name of the latest section of the city which the Italians have pre-empted. It is the old Aaron Burr estate at the southern edge of what used to be Greenwich Village. Thompson and Sullivan Sts., with those between Bleecker and MacDougal Sts., have few but Italian residents. Within six months Hancock Street has become Italian. High tenements are going up to replace the separate houses which once made this part of New York distinctively American.

Most of the residents of the "Richmond Hill" quarter are new arrivals. They found the East Side districts, both up and downtown, too crowded for comfort, and the stream from Southern Europe turned across Broadway. The men of the quarter are laborers and bootblacks, or they are lazy and do practically nothing. There are few garment workers, the women and children working on flowers and feathers.

"In no part of New York are the young children harder worked than in this district," said a resident of the settlement the other day. From three years of age until they are old enough to go into factories the children are forced to make pipe and cloth flowers in winter, and feathers for hat decoration in summer. The mother works at intervals between her housework, which is reduced to a minimum. The children are in schoolwork before and after. Even the older children who are employed in factories paste and twist flowers before breakfast and after they return at night. It matters not how tired they are or how unwilling to work. The mother or father is there with a stick, and necessity makes them hard taskmasters.

"A family where there are four or five children of working age can make as much as $6 a week out of flowers or feathers, according to the season. The average, however, is much less, say from $1 50 to $3.50 a week. This sum, with the husband's wages, enables them to live, if not in comfort. Because of the poverty the religious celebrations are not so extensive as in the East Side quarters.

"This home work is a great incentive to truancy, if not to keep the children out of school entirely. Just before Easter this year, when the rush for flowers was at its height, two of our kindergarten children did not appear. Thinking they might be ill, I visited the home and found the tots at work on cheap cloth violets.

The South to Get Them

" 'Do you want to work?' I asked. 'We has to,' ventured one of them with a fearsome look at the stick which his mother held."

From the Bureau of Immigration at Washington comes the report that all records in the number of aliens arriving in the United States have been broken by those of the fiscal year ending June 30. Heretofore the banner immigration year was 1882, when the total reached 785,992. The total for eleven months of this year was 758,285, and more than 100,000 arrived during the month of June. Of this Italians led all other nations. In May 37,733 subjects of King Victor Emmanuel III landed on these shores, an increase of 875 over the same month last year. No one can say when the influx will stop. The Roman Catholic Church, to which practically all of the Italians belong, is finding difficulty in ministering to their religious needs. It is said that arrangements are being made to bring no less than two hundred priests from Italy to work in the Italian parishes of Manhattan and Brooklyn. Three new Italian churches are planned for Brooklyn. In the region where these people have settled and in various parts of the city American churches are being given over to them.

The Irish Standard (Minneapolis)
May 5, 1906

The South to Get Them

European Immigrants Are Beginning to Learn That There is an America Outside of New York

Most of the New Comers of the Next Few Years Will Settle in States of the South and South-West

In Order to Encourage People to Settle in the South a Passenger Line to New Orleans is Planned

That the greater part of the vast army of immigrants which will come to America during the next few years will distribute itself over the agricultural states of the South and Southwest and there found a new race of sturdy, progressive Americans is the prediction made by Friedrich von Pills, a director of the North Herman Lloyd Steamship Company and one of the world's experts on the subject of immigration, says the New York Herald.

Throughout the continent of Europe the word has been spread, he asserts, that the cities of America, particularly New York and Chicago, are now filled to overflowing with foreigners, and with it has gone the tidings that the great agricultural states like Texas, Missouri, Mississippi and Louisiana hold out golden promise to the rugged alien whose life dream is a home of his own and enough acres to provide a comfortable livelihood for his family.

Hundreds of thousands of stalwart peasants of German blood from southern Russia, Bulgaria, Roumania and Hungary will flock to America, he declares, with their baggage checked straight through to distant points in the South and Southwest, and they will bring money enough to give them a fair start in the life they wish to lead. They will not come with the intention of returning after they have accumulated what in their native countries would be considered snug fortunes, but will leave home with the declared purpose of becoming American citizens and adopting American ideas. America, Mr. von Pills says, should not regard with alarm the incoming hordes of foreigners, but should welcome them, and should give a double welcome to the swarm of agriculturists which will come here in the next half dozen years. Any country in Europe, he says, would be sorry to lose them; every country should be glad to receive them as residents.

As managing director of the steerage department of his steamship line, Mr. Von Pills for more than a year has been conducting a campaign of education in the European countries which contribute to the immigrant horde. He has sent agents into the centers of population to tell the people that American cities offer few advantages to the foreigner, because they are already filled to overflowing, and has pointed out the opportunities in the great agricultural commonwealths which, in many parts, are still in a state of undevelopment. American consuls, he says, have aided in this work of education, and hundreds of thousands of letters from foreigners in America have opened the eyes of the restless Europeans. What should now be done, he says, to carry the plan to fulfillment is for the several slates which are anxious for emigrants to settle in them and work their farms, to establish bureaus in New York, enlighten the newcomers and direct them.

The South to Get Them

Studying in the South

To prevent further congestion in the cities of New York, Chicago, Philadelphia, Buffalo and Baltimore, the North German Lloyd Steamship Company is planning to start a new passenger line between Bremen and New Orleans and will sell tickets direct from the point of embarkation to cities and villages in the interior of the southern states, just as it now does over the line established a year ago to Galveston.

Mr. Von Pills is now in the South making inquiries concerning those sections which are most advantageous to the foreigners. He will return to New York in a week or ten days and will then depart for Germany to put into full operation the scheme he is perfecting. Although young in years, being but thirty-two, his long connection with the great steamship company and his previous service with the German government as colonizer for eastern Prussia have made him one of the foremost authorities on immigration.

Desiring to populate the thinly settled province of Posen, in eastern Prussia, the government selected him to undertake the work and in three years made a thriving agricultural region of the province, sending in Germans from Galicia, Hungary, Russia and Roumania. Completing this task, he became director of the steerage department of the North German Lloyd Steamship Company and in that capacity has visited all the corners of Europe, as well as South American countries and most of the American states.

"Is America to expect a million new residents from Europe every year?" he was asked.

"America may always expect to receive a big army of immigrants from Europe," he said, "but not a million a year. The high water mark has been reached. Last year established what probably always will be the record, although 1906 will see but a slight falling off. There were plenty of causes for the remarkable exodus from Europe last year and for the continued outpouring of the first few months of 1906. In the first place, the failure of the crop in Hungary in 1904 caused a great many Hungarians to emigrate to America, and the lack of settled government aided. The chief cause, however, was the political disturbances in Russia. But conditions have righted themselves in a large measure now, and henceforth there will be but a steady, healthy flow of Europeans to American shores.

"New York need not worry about the immigration of the future. The Europeans who come to America in the steerage are beginning to learn that there is an America that is not New York, and to realize that in the great stretches of country to the south and west there are limitless opportunities for the man of thrift who wishes to establish a home of his own and is willing to toil and thrive to do it. The great part of the army which will swarm into America in the next few years will check its baggage straight through the port of entry, be it New York, Philadelphia, Baltimore or Boston, and will pass on to the rich states which lie back of them.

"To practically every immigrant and to all their fellows at home America has always been New York. They picture a great swarming city, a little stretch of farmland and forest, and then—Chicago, Boston, Philadelphia, Pittsburg mean little to them—they have heard the names and they suggest factories and teeming hives of humanity. Little has the peasant population of Germany realized that Texas alone is larger than their entire country and that there are dozens of states of fertile soil uncultivated because there is no one to cultivate them.

"Two years ago I made my first trip to America in the interest of our steerage service and I then found that New York, Chicago, Boston, St. Louis, Kansas City and a dozen other cities were overcrowded with foreigners and that the tides of immigration should be directed to the rural sections of the country. The whole question was taken up by the management of the North German Lloyd Steamship Company, and as a result we established a line direct from Bremen to Galveston, Texas. Our first boat to that port carried fifteen immigrants; our last one, which landed only a few days ago, carried 1,100. To enable the immigrants to get to the interior of the country without trouble we arrange their transportation direct from Bremen to any inland destination.

"So successful has the service to Texas proved that I shall recommend on my return the establishment of a new line to New Orleans, this being the gateway to the great agricultural states of Louisiana, Georgia, Mississippi and Alabama. Nowhere so much as in the southern states should there be a desire to turn the streams of immigration into the South. Those states need good farmers and hundreds of thousands of them will arrive in America in the next few years. We have educated the prospective immigrants as well as we could and shall make every effort to direct them to the regions where they are needed and where they can reside with most profit to themselves, and I would suggest that the various states establish bureaus in New York and other ports of entry to aid in the work. Much could be accomplished in this way."

"From what part of Europe may America expect the greatest army of immigrants in the next few years?" he was asked.

"That is not easy to tell," he said. "Italy will continue to send a flood of aliens here. Italy, in fact, is the only European country which does not discourage wholesale emigration to America. Russia will continue to pour into your cities streams of Hebrews, but not so numerous as during the last two or three years, and Hungary will contribute her share.

"I would say. however, that the next flood will come from the German districts of southern Russia, Roumania, Bulgaria and Hungary, and they will be the kind of people that America ought to welcome with open arms, the type of rugged manhood that adds strength to any state. The people who are now turning their eyes to America are agriculturists, and I fully expect to see a great exodus of them to your shores. Some will go to South America, but the great mass will strike out for America, and their destination will not be the centres of population. They will want to cling to their occupation—that of tilling the soil. The German residents of the countries I have named are powerful men, of exemplary habits, and their idea of success in life is to have homes of their own and to rear healthy families.

"These people would a boon to the South. They are accustomed to temperature and soil much the same and would bring about an almost magical development of the great area which now lacks proper cultivation. They are natural farmers and hard workers. They will start a new race in the South—will be the new pioneers. Twenty years from now, I confidently predict, America will be glad she left her doors open and pointed the way to the land of the cotton fields

"There need be no fear in America that Europe us unloading upon her an undesirable population. It is quite true that many of the immigrants, notably from Italy, are not the best sort of citizens, but those who come from central Europe are the kind of people that Europe does not wish to lose. Many of those who come from Italy spend part of the year here and return to their homes with their American earnings. This is a custom which should be discouraged. But in the case of the people from Hungary, Bohemia, Roumania, Bulgaria and other parts of Europe, they emigrate for good. They sever all ties abroad and start out with the determination to link their fortunes with those of America and to send for their relatives as soon as they can scrape together sufficient money.

"Inspection at the point of embarkation is far more rigid than it has ever been, and it would doubtless surprise many people in your country to know how many thousands of people are sent back to their homes because they are not physically sound or because they would lie dependent as soon as they reached America. Why, at the port of Bremen alone last year the North German Lloyd Steamship Company rejected 10,000 applicants for transportation to America. In America you have the faculty of making citizens quickly and you may be sure that the hordes that are already laying plans to land on your shores will be greatly assimilated.

"In the number of Hebrews coming to America from Russia there will be a marked falling off. For several years the stream of Hebrews from Russian ports to Argentina has been swelling, and this year the number will be larger than ever. Argentina is extending her arms to European immigrants and would gladly welcome all those that set out for America. That government offered me some time ago an enormous tract of land in one of the most productive parts of the country on the condition that I would people it with good, rugged Europeans.

"Stories of the sweat shops in New York and of the teeming tenements, where light and air are not to be had, have caused thousands of Hebrews who were thinking of migrating to New York to change their minds. Many of them will go to Argentina; many will go to other parts of the world but a comparatively small proportion will come to America. Most of the Hebrews who do will settle in New York, Chicago, Philadelphia and St. Louis, because they are not fitted for agricultural pursuits.

"America need not be alarmed when they read that 100,000—or whatever the number might be—immigrants landed in New York in a certain month. America will absorb them just as she has absorbed the millions who have come heretofore. any of your most intellectual and influential citizens are descendants of the great mass of Irish peasants who flooded your gates back in the forties. Many also are descendants of the multitude of Germans who scattered broadcast over your states thirty odd years ago. In a very few years many of your leading men will be descendants of the Italians who started for America some fifteen years ago."

San Francisco Call
August 25, 1907

What Are Our Immigrants Worth in Dollars and Cents?

by Sydney A. Reeves, Former Professor of Steam and Hydraulic Engineering at Worcester Polytechnic Institute and Lecturer at Harvard

  Tales of murder, arson, blackmail and more horrifying crimes are clogging the newspapers nowadays. And with them comes again the ever new and ever old question, "Are the immigrant hordes that pour into America to blame?" Police Commissioner Bingham of New York outspokenly lays at the door of the immigrant the responsibility for the late outbreak of unspeakable crimes against little girls, and for this he has been harshly criticized in some quarters. In other circles there is in progress again a serious discussion as to the advisability of curbing the immigration flood. All of this leads up to the question of the immigrant, his value or his menace and his position in the social machine. The Sunday Call herewith presents a new light on the problem, "What are the immigrants worth in dollars and cents?"

  Current conversation and the periodical press are full of condemnation of our lax restriction of immigration. All the evils to which our country is heir are explained by the "undesirable horde" of aliens which is pressing into the land with ever increasing volume. The steady increase in criminality which has now become unquestioned is attributed to this "overflow" of the undesirable from the older countries, and these countries are accused of collusion with the steamship companies toward a promotion of the volume of migration. That portion of our citizens which is interested in the labor market is in chronic rebellion against this influx of cheap labor, destined to compete upon an un-American basis with American labor. Those of us who are interested in purity of politics see in the inflowing torrent a current supply of corruptibles upon whose votes political machines may be reared and supported.

  Upon every side arises this denunciation of immigration. Nor is it a recent phenomenon. Look up the literature of immigration and you will find the decade of 1840-1850 supplying its fair quota of "kicks" in goodly proportion to what our increased population puts forth today. For 60 years we, as a nation, regardless of whether our continent yet contained undeveloped territory, as in 1847, or undeveloped possibilities, as in 1907, have been objecting strenuously to immigration.

Meanwhile the immigration has been steadily increasing, except during the period of the civil war, and at the end of the 60 years we enjoy phenomenal prosperity.

There is an inconsistency here somewhere between the theories of the pessimists and the facts, and a big one, too.

What are the facts?

As to criminality, we can find none supporting the theory that in general immigration is of a criminal sort. Here and there may be found minor facts and figures on that side, it is true. The southern Italians, without question, are unusually illiterate and addicted to the settlement of differences by stiletto. So, too, are the mountaineers of American Tennessee. We even identify the Italians roughly with the Black Hand system of blackmail. The south Italians are but a small fraction of all immigration; the class of crimes to which they are prone is a minor one in our criminal records: the blackmail extorted by the Black Hand is but a drop in the bucket compared with the volume of extortion currently practiced by American businessmen, within and without the law, against American born victims.

Viewing the situation broadly, there is no decisive evidence pointing to the criminality of the average immigrant. There is much pointing to his superiority over the average native American in industry, sobriety and the patient toleration of adverse conditions without outbreak. Indeed, the most decided evidence on this point comes from Great Britain, which country complains that of all her immigrants the Americans are the most criminal, being three or four times as bad as the average of the rest and 10 times as bad as the Poles and Hungarians!

We do not conclude from this too hastily that America is ultra criminal. But we quote it to signify that he who seeks statistical support for anti-immigration views, doing it in sincerity and breadth, is apt to meet with sour comfort.

Our own conclusions are that the vast majority of immigrants are slightly above our American standards in industry, sobriety and patient self-restraint, though they are undoubtedly below us in initiative. They come from countries where unceasing toil is the price of life and where the get-rich

What Are Our Immigrants Worth in Dollars and Cents?

-quick microbe is virtually unknown. In their fatherlands drunkenness is a minor crime, whereas in Great Britain and America it is a major one. And as to patience under conditions inviting to revolt, America is proud of standing first among all the non-Latin peoples of the temperate zones in here promptness to resent publicly, by the passive rebellion of the strike, if not by actual violence, the presence of conditions unnecessarily hard. Our complaint against the immigrants must be that they are too patient and submissive for American standards, rather than that they are too violent and resentful.

As to illiteracy, it is true that the immigrants are below our standard. What of it? Education is a thing of itself, neither conducive to nor antagonistic to morality and happiness. It may be a powerful tool of both. But it is often used as an equally powerful tool against both. Our educated classes are not always the happiest ones. Our worst and biggest crooks are the educated ones.

In short, a man is of value to a country solely according to whether he produces more, of material or of morality, than he consumes. He may produce very little, yet if his wants are less than that little he is still a profitable investment for the nation. He may, on the other hand, apparently produce millions; yet if he consumes more than that, or if he undermines our standards of morality, or if he is found to produce actually much less than he apparently produces, he may be a great source of loss, in spite of his prominence and power.

To which class, then, belongs the average immigrant? Is he a producer or a dissipater of net wealth and morality? If the former, what is our immigration worth, net, to the nation?

Our answer, it must be explained, is based upon economic principles which are laid down in the writer's "Cost of Competition." The distinction between the net productive and the net dissipative classes is there portrayed with accuracy. It is too bulky to be more than suggested here. But once in mind it makes it obvious that the vast majority of immigrants belongs to the net productive class.

Indeed, they belong to the most productive class. They not only confine their efforts to purely productive lines, wasting very little time in bargaining over prices or ownership of property, but they do not discount their worth, as do many American-born producers, by indulgences in labor tyranny. The walking delegate is essentially an Americanism.

What, collectively, are these immigrants worth to us as a nation?

Reporting: Immigrants 1803-1931

The law says that a dead male adult constitutes a loss of $5,000 to his family. In this it strikes a rough average and draws no distinction of any sort between individuals. So it is hard to get at it in that way.

The average adult male immigrant (and half of our immigrants are of this sort) earns at least $300 per annum soon after his arrival. Rather, that is what he is paid. My estimates have led me to state, elsewhere, that his actual productivity is from three to four times that amount, the balance going to pay the cost of doing "business" with what he produces and consumes. But the benefit of this doubt will be left, for the present, to the opposition. We shall base our estimates upon the $300 figure.

The right will be reserved, however, to class all immigrants under this figure, for the majority of them have been here long enough to expand their income beyond $300. That is to say, most of those who were classed as children at the time of entry are now adults. Of the women, some are offset in their unproductivity by the men who earn more than $300; the rest are producing more than that value in the form of children.

During the last 20 years some sixteen or seventeen million immigrants have arrived. The exact figure does not matter, for all we wish is an estimate of the number now alive and working, and many who came before 1887 are that. If these people are producing an average of $300 worth of goods and children apiece their current productivity is now five billions of dollars per annum.

This is two hundred times as much as our new automobiles cost us last year. This enormous fund of current income we should have lost had we rigidly excluded immigration in 1887. It is some such sum as this which we are losing each year that we continue our exclusion of the oriental races.

How much capital do these immigrants embody, not in their pockets or bank accounts, but in their strength of body and character?

Assume that out of the 17,000,000 aliens arrived since 1887 10,000,000 are now adult males. For each one of these that you kill his family can collect from you, by law, $5,000. He must be worth at least half that. That is to say, we have got from Europe during the last two decades, for nothing, a working machine which capitalizes at from twenty-five to fifty billions!

This figure agrees fairly well with our estimate of the annual productivity of this great human machine. But this exactness of the figures does not matter. It is plain that, however they may be modified in detail, they will still remain enormous. Our crops have certainly been enormous

What Are Our Immigrants Worth in Dollars and Cents?

of recent years, but it has already become plain that they cannot stand alone as an explanation of our remarkable prosperity. We not only grow hundreds of millions of dollars' worth of corn, wheat and cotton, at the cost of much labor each year, but we also imbibe with another continent, without a cent of cost to ourselves, upward of a billion dollars' worth of human livestock per annum.

This last statement is based upon the supposition that the average value of an immigrant, including the minority of females and boys, is only $1,000 at the time of entry. And certainly, when we recall the average price of a sound negro slave in the days before the war, in such a condition that would pass our immigration inspectors, and allow for the greater efficiency of the modern industrial organization over the plantation gang of negroes fresh from mid-Africa, this figure of $1,000 apiece is moderate.

We do not hesitate to assign a solid value to every other form of livestock which the land needs for its working. Why should not our immigrants be figured as a similar asset?

The immigration officials lost a fine chance to be human when they failed to christen "Welcome!" the ferry boat which plies between Ellis Island and the Battery, and which waves the American flag for the first time above most of these homeless ones. The name should have been emblazoned on the boat in every language known to Europe.

It would have taken considerable altruism, considerable height and breadth of thought, considerable courageous disregard of prevailing phariseeism, to have done this. It was hardly to be expected that mere men should have risen to such a height. And yet, had it been done, should we not have had to look upon the deed a little shamefacedly? More than a billion of good, exploitable capital, capable of producing a current income of a fifth of that sum each year, coming into the country each year for nothing, and we have the courage to stand up and say "Welcome!" openly? Indeed not! We know our own dignity too well for that! Let us continue to insist that it is as a favor that we condescend to accept it.

by Robert Watchorn, Commissioner of Immigration

Public opinion is all wrong, or nearly so, upon many phases of the immigration question. With more than a million immigrants a year we cannot supply the urgent demands for labor. The menace of pauper immigrants is a myth. This army of workers adds enormously to the wealth and prosperity of the country.

It is not the scum of Europe we are getting, but the pick of the most earnest and hard working of its population. As to the morality of the immigrants of today, it seems to me that it compares favorably with that of our native-born population.

This is not a matter of mere opinion or sentiment. It is borne out by the actual statistics. Mr. Reeves' figures, it seems to me, in some respects understate the facts. He mentions $300 a year as the earning power of these immigrants. As a matter of fact these men will earn more, on the average, than a dollar a day. I think the figure may safely be increased by at least 50 per cent. Within a few days Charles W. Lorhn, the New York state commissioner of labor, came to me in search of men I could not supply. He estimated that New York state alone needed 100,000 men, to whom he would pay $25 a month and board on the farms alone. Now, that does not look much like overcrowding or the impossibility of assimilating we hear so much about.

Of the million, or, to be exact, the 1,004,756, immigrants last year more than 10 per cent were under 14 years, 4 per cent were over the age limit and a great proportion brought their wives. About 50 per cent may be classed as workers. But in another sense they were all workers. There were no idlers, scarcely one who would shirk his duty. And as to their morality, the average is certainly good. These immigrants are placed upon a probation for three years. Should they get into trouble in this time they are liable to be deported. Last year there were for all causes less than 1,200 deported. I question if our native born population can show a better record.

The modern immigrant of today, it seems to me, is greatly misunderstood. We hear a great deal of talk about the menace of the immigrant from the south of Europe. A few decades ago most of the immigrants came from Ireland, while Germany ranked second and Great Britain third. Italy and Russia sent comparatively few. Today the situation is practically reversed. Last year we received 267,000 from Italy, 192,000 from Russia and but 24,000 from Ireland and 30,000 from Germany. From Austria and Hungary some 292,000 reached our shores. It is unfair to say that the north of Europe is no longer represented. But are the immigrants from the southern countries dangerous or undesirable? The statistics of crime do not prove it. The Italian is a hard worker. We should remember that the Latin

What Are Our Immigrants Worth in Dollars and Cents?

people were highly civilized when the north of Europe was peopled with savages. The southern countries may not have progressed of late, but the impulse is still there, and with unlimited opportunities of America before them who can tell what they may not accomplish in the future?

A great deal of the misunderstanding is due to the use of that term pauper labor. I have estimated that every immigrant in coming to America spends on an average from $80 to $100 for transportation. This includes his fare from his home to the point of departure, the crossing of the Atlantic and the railroad fare to his destination. In other words, they spend upward of $100,000,000 a year in search of work. Let us suppose for the sake of argument that Russia suddenly held out great opportunities for money making so that Americans by the millions were attracted there. It seems to me that 1,000,000 native born citizens might have some difficulty in raising $100,000,000 for transportation. And in addition, this army of incomers carried with them more than $20,000,000 in cash.

There is, of course, urgent need of the restriction of immigration, but such restriction is already in force. The laws governing the situation are very rigid; they have been devised by intelligent men, familiar with the situation, working in sympathy with these people as well as in the best interests of the country. And the laws are being enforced. As the need for further restriction occurs it will receive due attention. Meanwhile the demand for laborers throughout the country is very urgent. The immigrants are adding hundreds of millions of dollars to the wealth of America, while they help themselves to a broader and more prosperous life.

*by Emerson McMillan, Chairman,
Conciliatory Committee of the New York Civic Federation*

Decidedly I favor an intelligent restriction of immigration on both our eastern and western seaboards. Without being an alarmist, I venture to say that the problem grows more difficult each year and must ultimately demand a solution. America has accomplished wonders in assimilating great hordes of immigrants from many different countries, but it is a very serious question how long, at the present rate of increase, she can continue to do so. Now it seems to me that when foreigners come to us in such numbers that they form separate and distinct communities; preserving their language and traditions intact, they constitute a menace. When such a colony is formed it is difficult to break up. Assimilation goes on very slowly. Then, again, the class of immigrants who come to us has changed of late years. Formerly a great majority of these immigrants came from the north of Europe, from England, Germany, Norway, Sweden and Ireland. Today they come for the most part from southern countries, and, generally speaking, are less desirable. We may have great sympathy, for instance, for the Russian Jew in his sufferings, but when he comes to us in surprising numbers he becomes a problem. As a rule, the immigrant of recent years differs from us widely in his ideas of morality, his attitude toward the law and in his general point of view.

When we read of the violent crimes committed, the names are usually foreign. The "Black Hand" outrages, for instance, have doubtless been greatly exaggerated, but such as they are they are a foreign importation and of very recent years.

It is undeniable, of course, that the coming of these millions of laborers has contributed much to the wealth and prosperity of the country. But should this army of workers be increased indefinitely? We have a population today in excess of 80,000,000 very active and alert people. It would seem that the natural resources of the country could be developed and the great business of the land be carried forward very well with our present population and its natural increase. And I am not among those who have any fear of race suicide. The increase in the number of immigrants from year to year is astonishing. Can we continue to receive this army indefinitely without some day reducing our scale of income to that of Europe?

I remember very distinctly when the labor of the country, the digging and carrying, was done by the Irish almost exclusively. Well, today all this is changed. The Irish are still here, but they have prospered. They have become Americans and in turn are employing still other immigrants to do the rougher work of the land. Does it seem probable that the Slavs, the Russian Jews, the Sicilians and others who are coming to us in such numbers today will in a few years have risen as have the Irish, and have become as good Americans? And if these foreigners with traditions and manners very different from our own are not assimilated, the problem becomes a very serious one. Will the class of immigrants who are now coming to us some day become the same forceful, patriotic citizens as the natives of northern Europe who came a few decades ago? On the other hand, they may never be completely assimilated, or, at least, so slowly that in the process they will destroy our laws and transform the general attitude toward many American traditions. This argument applies particularly to the Chinese, and therefore I approve of the exclusion of the Chinese from our shores. The situation on the eastern seaboard of America, it seems to me, demands similar if less drastic measures.

Pacific Commercial Advertiser
March 16, 1908

Honolulu's Highways and Byways– Among the Opium Dens of Chinatown

Many Whites Among the Smokers—The Kodak Drives All to Cover

Fifty white men in Honolulu "hit the pipe" in the opium dives that exist to the number of a score or so in the heart of Chinatown. So one of the Chinese habitués of the joints informed an Advertiser investigator last week. And from the look of the joint where the information was given it was rather easy to believe that any white man who would go there would do anything. This place was in the rear of the row of dirty tenements facing Mauka on Pauahi street, near River. Every room in the back of that building on the ground floor except one is an opium joint and on the day of the visit was crowded with Chinese, many of whom were busily inhaling the white fumes from the burning dope or sleeping off their debauches. Tucked away in the corners of bunks, laid out on mats on the floor and even slid out of the limited way under the bunks were poppy-soaked figures, pallid-faced, and in many instances bare-footed and ragged, deep in sleep, dreaming of Elysium, while over and about them swarmed the teeming other patrons and proprietors of the dives.

There were no white men there, at least in evidence. White dope fiends do not expose themselves in the careless way that the Chinese do. Some of them have a remnant of shame left and seek the upper rooms of the dives on their visits, while all of them endeavor to keep out of the way of the police, who pay domiciliary calls very frequently to these places. Chinamen can smoke and drug themselves as they will, but the police arrest whites and Hawaiians found in these joints and lock them up for vagrancy. Then the deprivation of the drug proves to be a thousand times more punishment for them than all the other penalties the magistrate can impose.

There is nothing attractive about an opium dive. Dark, stinking with the exhalations of those who overcrowd the little rooms, floors and windows dirt-begrimed and filthy, and everywhere the reek and gurgle of the opium, there is nothing to remind the casual visitor of the fairy tales that are sometimes related of the palaces of Nirvana, where amid Oriental splendor the white slaves of the drug indulge themselves in vice. As a matter of fact the opium fiends among the whites are less fastidious than the Chinese themselves and with even less excuse. The photograph published herewith of the entrances to the dives in the one particular building gives but a faint conception of the squalor of the place. Prior to the exposure of the camera this alley was full of Chinamen, professional gamblers and others, who ducked for cover as soon as it was seen that a picture was to be taken. It is from among these men that the highbinder class is recruited, sneak thieves bred and criminals made. Most of them are opium smokers, spending their time playing games in the reeking joints during the day, the losing players paying for the pills for the winners. At night they pit their skill against that of the more industrious of their countrymen, fleecing them at the pai-kau or fan-tan tables. All of them are known to the police.

Throughout Chinatown there is scarcely a tenement in which at any time of the day or night some opium smoking is not going on, more or less publicly, and yet the vice is on the decline, or supposed to be. Quite recently an association was formed among the Honolulu Chinese to work for the suppression of opium. Many habitual smokers joined and announced that the drug was to be given up. The recipe for some especially noxious tasting brew was distributed around among the smokers and the medicine when taken regularly was guaranteed to cure the habit and stop the poppy-craving within three months. Many Chinamen began to use it, encouraged in their endeavor to break themselves of the habit by their consul. A good many of them claimed that the dope was actually lessening their desire for the pipe and the demand for the treacly stuff began to fall off. Perhaps it may be unjust to say that the dealers in opium and the proprietors of the dives were responsible, but at any rate about ten days ago a report began to circulate among the Chinese that certain death awaited the ones who persisted in taking this opium antidote. The report, which spread like wildfire among the Chinese, was that news had been received from China that those who had attempted to cure themselves of opium smoking in this way had all died suddenly within three months after beginning the treatment. Throughout the city the antidote was hurriedly spilled into sinks or poured out into back yards and many hundreds of extra punks smoked in propitiation before grinning josses. But hitting the pipe is decreasing because the number of old Chinamen in Honolulu is decreasing. The Hawaiian-Chinese do not to any number indulge in the vice.

This is not because they do not have plenty of opportunity to see plenty of it. In the very thickest of the hop joint section, in the building shown in the pictures here given, a score of bright-eyed little chaps attend a private school. The contrast between the joints downstairs and the little hall of learning upstairs is great. On the one hand grime, slothfulness and vice; on the other tidiness, youth and industry. Below, pigtails and talon-like finger nails; above, closely cropped polls and chubby fists curved to top spinning and marbles. The boys attend this school after the hours of the public schools. They will all be voters here some day.

Down at Pearl City, just across the track from the railroad station, there is a Chinese school in the front room and just through the open door are an opium joint and an opium pipe repairing shop. While at their noisy classes these children can see the dopesters at work.

Chinese Athletics

But all opium smokers are not Chinese: neither are all Chinese opium smokers, even among the older ones. Just as many of the young Chinese engage in Occidental sports and train their muscles for field and track contests, so the older ones, some of them, keep up their training along the methods brought with them from China. These methods are heroic and startling and the results are amazing. A course of exercises that will enable a man in the end to poke his forefinger through a half inch board or crack open a cocoanut with his fist amount to something, for their freakishness if for nothing else. There are some Chinamen who can do these things. Others harden the muscles of the forearm by whacking them with sticks, giving themselves welts from wrist to elbow that would black and blue the haole athlete to a pulp.

To secure photographs of some of these now old men in action is almost impossible. They do their stunts willingly enough for the one who cares to look them up, but their training quarters and gymnasiums are tucked away in cellars or darkened back rooms where snapshotting is impossible and they will not come out into the sunlight and face a camera. One was found the other day who was less modest. This is Pak Chew, who is well known to the police as a scrapper, one whose strength and skill are supposed to be at the disposal of the highest bidder and who figures generally on one side or the other in most of the tong mixups in the quarter. Unofficially he dropped in the other day to see his acquaintances at the police station and posed proudly for his picture.

His particular stunt is to invite anyone who wants to make a punching bag out of his stomach. By constant exercise of the abdominal muscles he has so strengthened these that the hardest puncher cannot even make a dent. Joe Leal, the assistant chief of detectives, failed even to stagger him. Barney Joy once undertook to knock the wind out of the Chink and bruised his knuckles, and many of the strong men and pugilists of the city have had like experience with "The Man with the Rubber Stomach," as Pak Chew delights in being called.

Congested Conditions

Throughout that section of the city between Nuuanu, and River, and King, and Beretania, each block is a perfect network of connecting buildings. Back in the centers of these blocks only enough ground is left unbuilt on to allow little alleyways, over which, from the second stories and roofs runways back and forth connect the buildings and provide plenty of get-away whenever the police descend on the inmates. These runways are principally used by the Chinese, and their buildings are the ones the most liberally provided with exits. Japanese and Hawaiians share their quarters but do not share their dislike of traveling on the ground when it can be avoided. They all seem to share the dislike for the Kodak, though, and several attempts to secure a picture in and around the swarming tenements only succeeded in driving everyone hurriedly indoors. A snapshot given here in one of the most congested blocks shows only apparently deserted lanais, although at least fifty Chinese men and women were busied on these same lanais less than one minute before the camera was snapped. The first sight of the picture machine sent them piling helter-skelter behind the slammed doors.

Los Angeles Herald
January 17, 1909

Is the Famous Italian "Black Hand" Organization a Myth?

No Deep-Dyed Body of Italians, Say Prominent Men, to Conduct Organized Blackmail and Murder

Nearly 500,000 Italians in New York and but Forty Policemen Speak the Italian Language

SCARCELY a day passes without some mention coming up in the news of the misdoings of "The Black Hand Organization." Either it is a "Black Hand Robbery," "A Black Hand Kidnapping" or "A Black Hand Dynamiter," and sometimes even "A Black Hand Murder." Reports of "The Black Hand Society" have been so constant and so recurrent that the whole country is kept in a state of continuous alarm. Now the question has come up, somewhat paradoxically at first it seems, "Is there actually such a criminal organization of Italians operating together and known as The Black Hand?" Prominent Italians in New York City and elsewhere, and those also in a position to most know, scoff at the idea, and deny without exception that such a society exists.

"In the United States, 'The Black Hand' is a myth, in so far as the phrase conveys the impression that an organization of Italians exists in America, or that the Camorra or the Mafia has been naturalized," Gaetano D'Amato, former president of the United Italian Societies, wrote in a recent issue of the North American Review.

Police Sergeant Petrosino, in charge of the Italian Bureau at headquarters, recently said: "As far as they can be traced, threatening letters are generally a hoax; some of them are attempts at blackmail by inexperienced criminals, who have the idea suggested to them by reading about 'the Black Hand' in the sensational papers, but the number of threatening letters sent with the deliberate intention of using violence as a last resort to extort money is ridiculously small."

Baron E. Edmond Mayor des Planches, Ambassador to the United States from Italy, who more than anyone else knows the conditions of Italians in America and who is dean of the Diplomatic Corps in Washington, has repeatedly announced that he does not believe that in the United States there exists an organization of criminal Italians operating from any central agency, like "the Black Hand," and Dr. G. E. Di Palma Castiglione, of the Labor Information Office for Italians, who is in touch every day in the week with Italian immigrants of all classes, says:— "As an organization the Black Hand is non-existent. Its sole existence, in fact, is confined to a literary phrase, which has, I grant, so compelling and terrible a symbolism that one must almost believe it really exists when one only hears the phrase 'Black Hand.'" The report of the Commissioner General of Immigration, Frank P. Sargent, in 1904, contained a study of aliens who at that time were inmates in the various public institutions in the United States. The total number of alien inmates was 44,983 and of this number only 3,266 were Italians. In the penal institutions there was confined 1,318 Italians, as against 9,525 other aliens. In the insane asylums there were 719 Italians, as against 19,764 other aliens, and in the various charitable institutions there were 1,230 Italians, as against 15,395 other aliens. Of the 1,318 Italians in the penal institutions, 755 were incarcerated charged with grave crimes and 563 were incarcerated charged with minor crimes.

THESE figures have been given to indicate the unfairness of making the Italians as a race suffer for the crimes of their proportionately few criminals. Those who have been arrested tor being members of the "Black Hand" organization really are independent malefactors, who might happen to be socially intimate; they might frequent the same cafe, or they might occasionally meet together over a game of cards, but these meetings are a matter of chance and accidental more than the result of the workings of any criminal organization. In grave crimes two or three of these independent Italian desperadoes might band together, but not because they are members of any criminal organization, but because this

Is the Famous Italian "Black Hand" Organization a Myth?

is a common practice among criminals of all kinds, Americans as well as Italians.

There are many Italian criminals in this country. Prominent Italians admit this, and they blame the federal government for permitting so many of them to enter. In Italy there are two laws which prohibit the mayor of any city from issuing passports to criminals if they have committed a crime which would make them liable to disbarment in the United States by the immigration officials. No Italian, they say, should be permitted to enter the United States until his penal certificate has been examined. Yet there is no examination of the papers of immigrants of any kind at Ellis Island. If he has committed no crime in Italy the penal certificate will be blank. If the certificate is not blank the immigration authorities should deport him at once to Italy.

According to the federal laws, any person may be deported who has been convicted of a felony or any other crime involving "moral turpitude." The federal government as yet has no precise category of crimes which in its opinion involve "moral turpitude." Conscious of this defect in the immigration laws of the United States, the Italian government has requested the federal government to specify which crimes involve "moral turpitude," as the phrase is a vague one. In Turkey an Armenian may be looked upon as a criminal; elsewhere he might be considered as some kind of a hero.

Up to the present time the federal government has given no answer to the Italian government. It is said in Washington that the decision must be left entirely to the judgment of the immigration officers who examine the incoming immigrant. "The Italian government does its best to prevent the departure of criminals for America," Mr. Castiglione of the Labor Information Office for Italians said. "There are a number of Italians who leave Italy not from Italian ports but from French and German ports. The Italian government, of course, cannot reach those, because it has no jurisdiction over them. The Italian criminals in this country are to be found among the Italians who come without passports—that is to say, from non-Italian ports."

Prominent Italians in New York City and elsewhere complain that every European of dark complexion, unless he wears a Turkish fez when arrested, is put down on the police blotter as being an Italian and in this way the Italians are made responsible for crimes committed by other nationalities. An anecdote has been going the rounds of the Italian bankers in New York City of how a well known Italian merchant of Hoboken, Mr. Blanchetti by name, was pictured by an enterprising journalist as being one of the assassins involved in the murder of King Humbert. This picture was copied in all the papers throughout America; it eventually found its way into the Italian newspapers in this country, and it was then copied by newspapers in Italy. Mr. Blanchetti, an honored and respected man, soon lost all his friends and his business decreased; he died within a year, his acquaintances said, of a broken heart.

NEW YORK city contains anywhere from 500,000 to 700,000 Italians, yet there are only forty policemen in the Police Department who either speak the Italian language or are themselves Italians. In the city of Naples, which contains about the same number of Italians as does New York City, no more, there are approximately two thousand policemen, which includes the carabinieri, the soldier police. Two to three hundred policemen, who, if they are not themselves Italians, should at least be able to speak the Italian language, are necessary to keep this large Italian population under authority, say the prominent New York Italians.

"The Black Hand has scarcely even been heard of in Italy," Gaetano d'Amato says, and he quotes from the writings of an English criminologist, A. F. Griffiths, to prove that the Black Hand is not only a Spanish organization but that it had its origin in Spain. He contends that individual Italian criminals in this country on hearing the name the Black Hand were fascinated with its terrible symbolism, and they adopted it; it spread eventually to Italy. These criminals employed it because it acted on the receiver the same as the name of a well known author acts on the judgment of an editor, one Italian banker illustrated to the writer.

The only criminal organization in Italy is the Camorra, and the Camorra exists only in the city of Naples. The poverty of Naples has been responsible for its creation, as the Camorra is a sort of criminal collection agency. Almost the only way a usurer's debt can be collected in Naples is through the co-operation of the Camorra, because the people of the city are so poor that a judgment from the courts is valueless. The Camorra has its chiefs, its offices and its officers, and it is made up of ruffians, "cadets," protectors of usurers and adventurers in general. Of course these criminals

Is the Famous Italian "Black Hand" Organization a Myth?

belonging to the Camorra do far more desperate things than collect debts. The Mafia is not an organization, but, like the Kentucky feuds, it is rather a spirit of revenge, and perhaps it is less cruel than the feuds of the Kentucky mountaineers, for it at least stops at the grave.

All Italians who come from the southern part of Italy or Sicily are looked upon either as being members of the "The Black Hand" or "The Mafia" or some other criminal society, yet of the 1,197,552 persons who migrated from Italy during the years 1904 and 1905 only 6,000 were Neapolitans, and all certainly did not come to the United States. Some went to South America and Canada, and others went to Australia and other countries.

In the report made by Miss Emily Fogg Meade for the federal government, published in the Bulletin of Labor, May, 1907, is given an account of the rise and growth of the Italian colony at Hammonton, Atlantic County, N. J. This town, which numbers now between four and five thousand, has. been built up almost entirely by Sicilians. Miss Meade praises the Sicilians as fruit growers and as farmers, and in general has nothing but praise for their temperance and industry. She indicates that in 1906-7 they paid $4,493.67 taxes in Hammonton, and that there were 1,370 names of Sicilians and southern Italians on the tax register. In her report it is stated that nearly every week or so a house is built between Rosedale and Winslow by some Sicilian.

"The Italians of Hammonton show themselves to be a social people with simple, natural tastes," she says; "their love of home and children is healthful. They are ignorant, primitive, childlike, but their faults will largely be mended by contact with good American customs. Their courtesy, gentleness and love of outdoor life and simple pleasures are actual contributions to American life. The country environment seems to develop their better qualities and they take a normal part in the life of the community." Miss Meade's general summing up of the colony of Sicilians and southern Italians in Hammonton is as follows:—"In Hammonton are found the results of twenty years' contact of a typical American population with the lowest class of Sicilian immigrants. It is a safe conclusion that what the Italian has been able to accomplish in Hammonton he can achieve elsewhere under similar circumstances..."

ALL over the country prominent Italians are surprised that the immigration authorities and the police departments of the various cities do not more thoroughly inform themselves in reference to the facts about the so-called "Black Hand Society."

"There is no doubt that among the two million or more Italians living in the United States there are many criminals," Mr. Castiglione said, "and if journalists would confine themselves to studying the especial characteristics of Italian criminals it would be legitimate, but so many unscientific and uninformed writers strike not only at the Italian criminals, but at Italians themselves, and for no other reason than that they are Italians.

"The 'Black Hand' is not a tree spreading its roots deeper and deeper in the national life of the United States, as so many hysterical writers have affirmed. It is not a closely woven system, as others have written. It is only a general name appropriated by individual Italian criminals, under which they hide their own wrongdoings.

"The publication of these hastily prepared and sensational articles is an offence against American common sense and against the Italian American citizens. Articles of this kind powerfully contribute to the creating of an unfair feeling all over the country against a large part of the Italian population. These stories circulate not only in the larger cities, where the readers are more sophisticated, but they filter their way into the interior of the country, into the smaller towns, and are read by the gentle and peaceful farmers.

"These simple-minded readers believe firmly that every word printed in these articles is correct, that the stories are founded on fact, and in every Italian they meet, even if it be only a poor worn out laborer with his dinner pail, they see a "Black Hand' member. And if in these portions of the country there are no Italians the residents take steps to prevent any from ever settling there.

"Is it fair to the Italians, is it useful for this country that this feeling should be created and spread among its citizens?" Mr. Castiglione continued. "Of the two million Italians in the United States many have taken out their papers and become naturalized Americans. Many of them have settled here with their families, are sending their children to American schools, are investing their savings in American real estate, in American industries, in American business enterprises. In the city of New York alone conservative estimates place the value of real estate owned by Italians at twenty millions of dollars."

Gaetano D'Amato, in his North American Review article, places the wealth of the Italians of the United States, and which he says has all been earned within the last twenty-five years, as follows: property, $120,000,000; invested in wholesale commerce, $100,000,000; real estate, $50,000,000; deposits in local banks, $20,000,000.

The large majority of the Italians work hard to build the subways, to ditch the sewers, and they are obliged for the limited wages they receive to live in slums where many of them contract tuberculosis and other dreaded diseases. Others are building the railroads, excavating the canals, and they live in labor camps far from any civilization, sleeping in shanties, nourishing themselves with poor food. Still others are working in the mines, the quarries, risking their lives every moment of every day, without practically any protection of the law in case of accident. Many Italians devote themselves to agriculture. Prosperous agricultural colonies are lo be found in Vineland, N. J.; Tentitown, Ark., and St. Helena, N. C. In California Italians own and cultivate the largest and finest vineyards in the United States. In Louisiana many Italians are working in the cottonfields and in sugar plantations.

"Is it fair to arouse a national feeling against them, and only because some of them (and the statistics eloquently show how proportionately few) are criminals? It is unfair not only to the Italian race, but it is even dangerous to America and Americans," Mr. Castiglione said.

It is quite evident that so long as credence is given by the papers and the American public at large to the stories relating to the so-called "Black Hand" organization individual Italian criminals will be encouraged to continue keeping up their delusion, for by doing so they hide their own crimes behind the phrase "the Black Hand."

"AMERICA is still in need of settlers," Mr. Castiglione continued. "Large tracts of its territory must yet be cultivated. In arousing a feeling of disgust and fear against Italians many sections of the country are prevented from using them in the development of their natural resources. A few months ago the legislature of the state of Virginia passed a resolution the aim of which was to prevent the settlement of Italians in Virginia. In 1907 in North Carolina, there was also some legislation enacted to this effect, and yet in St. Helena (the same state) there is a flourishing settlement of Italians. They have their own church, co-operative store, bake oven, blacksmith shop, and they have designed and built all these buildings themselves. The southern newspapers time and time again have featured and written up the virtues and progress of the Italian colonists at St. Helena, N C."

The usual impression is that America gets "the scum of Italy." It is significant that only one and one-half per cent of Italian immigrants are debarred by the immigration officers. The Italian immigrants are usually strong, healthy and able-bodied, their ages varying from twenty to thirty-five years. These immigrants never become paupers. Mr. James Forbes, chief of the mendicancy department of the Charity Organization Society, says he has never seen or heard of an Italian tramp. Detective Sergeant Petrosino says he has never seen or heard of an Italian woman "on the street," and Miss Meade in her government report praises the chastity of the Sicilian women in Hammonton, N J.

Although the Italians drink considerable of their own light wines, they yet are a temperate race. John Foster Carr says: "With the exception of the Russian Jews, the Italians are by far the most sober of all nationalities." James J. Starrow, of Boston, says in a recent article: "The Italian drunkard hardly exists."

"So far from being the scum of Italy's paupers and criminals, our Italian immigrants are the very flower of her peasantry," John Foster Carr said in a recent article in The Outlook. "They bring healthy bodies and a prodigious will to work. They have an intense love for their fatherland and a fondness for old customs, and both are deepened by the hostility they meet and the gloom of the tenements they are forced to inhabit. The sunshine, the simplicity, the happiness of the old ways are gone, and often you will hear the words, "Non c'è placere nella vita" (There is no pleasure in life here). But yet they come, driven from a land of starvation to a land of plenty. Each year about one-third of the great host of the industrial recruits from Italy, breaking up as it lands into little groups of twos and threes and invading the tenements almost unnoticed, settle in the different colonies of New York. New York tenement houses are not adapted to life as it is organized in the hill villages of Italy, and a change has come over every relation of life. The crowded living is strange and depressing. Instead of work accompanied by song in orangeries and vineyards there is silent toil in the canyons of a city street; instead of the splendid and expostulating carabiniere there is the rough force of the New York policeman to represent authority."

New York Tribune
March 14, 1909

Detective Pelosino Black Hand Victim

Slain in Sicily While on Secret Mission

Italian Sleuth's Work to Go On with Even Greater Vigor— All Cities Asked to Help Local Police

Palermo, Sicily. March 13. — Lieutenant Joseph Petrosino, head of the Italian squad of the New York Police Department, was shot to death at 9 o'clock last evening under the shadow of the trees of Marina Square, in this city. Whether he was lured there or not is unknown, but it is believed that Petrosino, who during his stay in Sicily had been indefatigable in searching up the records of Sicilian criminals, had gone to the square in the hope of getting information which he considered of the utmost importance.

The identity of the assassins has not been disclosed, for they made their escape after having assured themselves of the death of the detective. Not the slightest trace of them has yet been discovered, but undoubtedly they were men who had reason to dread Petrosino's presence in Italy, either because he was on their traces or on the tracks of fellow members of some of the secret organizations in America. Petrosino had managed to collect while here much evidence of the criminality of a large number of Italians who have taken refuge in the United States, which would have given the American government the power to deport them. In a number of cases Petrosino had traced murder to their hands. His work will be largely destroyed by his death, as he had not had the time tor the opportunity to place much of his data on record.

His assassination was a most cold-blooded one. He was attacked in the darkness at the corner of the deserted square by two men, who fired three shots at him. Petrosino, though mortally wounded, clung desperately to life and showed at the very last moment extraordinary courage and coolness. Though the blood was streaming from him and he could feel that death was near, he clung with one hand to the grating of a nearby window,

He managed to draw his revolver and fire one shot and then fell to the ground. His bullet missed its mark, but the noise of the explosion attracted several persons. The first of these was a sailor from the warship Calabria, who as he ran up saw the detective dragging himself to his feet and grasping the iron bar with nerveless hand, but as the sailor reached him Petrosino fell again to the ground covered with blood, which was flowing from a desperate wound in the face. His eyes were still staring as, in a last effort to defend himself, he turned, revolver in hand, to where his assailants had been. He was dead before the sailor and others who went to his assistance could raise his head.

A magistrate, who was informed of the assassination, went immediately to the spot and ordered the body searched for identification. The identity of the murdered man was at once disclosed. From papers found on him it seems that he had been gathering evidence with reference to Italian criminals in the United States. There were also notes concerning the Palermo members of the Black Hand. Several postal cards were found addressed to his wife, "Adelina Petrosino, No. 223 Lafayette Street, New York," and a metal badge, No. 285.

From other papers found on the body it seems that Petrosino had made a tour of Sicily, and had given special attention to Trapani. The magistrate gave orders that the body be transported to Rotalli Cemetery, where a post-mortem was held.

The first official news of the assassination received by the police in this city came from William H. Bishop, the American consul at Palermo. The cable dispatch said:

Petrosino shot. Instantly killed in heart of city this evening. Assassin unknown. Dies a martyr.

BISHOP, *Consul,*
Palermo, Italy.

That "Joe" Petrosino had been shot and killed in the Fatherland was known early yesterday morning in "Little Italy." Not in years has there been as much excitement there. Italians discussed the murder on corners and in the cafes, and while some showed sorrow there were others who gloated over the death of the Italian detective. In the little cafes where they eat spaghetti and drink Chianti nothing else was talked of last night, and as the "red ink" flowed faster and faster the tongues of some of the diners were loosened, but if one spoke too loudly of Petrosino and his foul killing he was hushed up by his steadier neighbor.

A stranger in one of the cafes last night was an unwelcome guest, for as soon as the news of Petrosino's death reached here a swarm of detectives from the Central Office spread over the whole Italian district, delving into nooks and corners for some slip of the tongue that might tell who "got" "Joe" Petrosino.

Petrosino met his death only a few weeks after the killing of "Jack" Goldhammer, a side partner in the ferreting out of crime in this city. Yesterday the police were boiling over with anger.

Central Office detectives late last night arrested three Italians and lodged them in cells at police headquarters, all charged with carrying concealed weapons in violation of one of the sections of the Penaal Code, which makes the offence a felony.

The shooting of Petrosino in the land of his birth will not go unavenged. The Italian sleuth had no chance in his native country, where he was surrounded by spies of the societies that have worked their blackmailing schemes for years. He had no side partner to give a resounding rap of the nightstick on the pavement to tell him there was trouble in the air. He died alone, with no one to help him, in a country where his gold shield meant nothing.

Favorite Among Policemen

Up at police headquarters, the news of the murder of the chief of the special secret detective squad was received at first with scoffing, then amazement and then anger. Not only at headquarters, but among the policemen all over the city, the same bitter anger and resentment was shown, for Petrosino was a great favorite among his brothers.

Petrosino's death will mean a fiercer warfare on the Italian societies in this city which prey upon Italians and extort money from them by threatening letters. Lieutenant Petrosino met his end through his energy in hounding these criminals, but there will be others to take up the work where he left off. Deputy Commissioner Woods said yesterday: "The police department can give no information at all as to the purpose of Lieutenant Joseph Petrosino's visit to Italy and to other places he had been in. This is a matter of detective work and will not stop because of the death of one man. It would be hard to overestimate the value of Lieutenant Petrosino's work. Besides being a skillful detective, he was an honest, reliable, man and had the full respect of everyone. Devotion to duty and utter disregard of personal consequences have always been characteristic of him.

"It is hoped that the assassination of this faithful servant of New York City may bring home to people some idea of the seriousness of the Black Hand situation. Although the number of Black Hand crimes has been decreased about 50 percent in the last few months, it is impossible to make any radical move against these outlaws unless the police department can have the use of a secret service fund provided by the city, and unless congress will pass immigration laws which will keep criminals out and make it possible to put out any that may slip in. The immigration laws today, as far as they affect the entrance of criminals into this country, are such a short way that they almost entirely fail in accomplishing the object intended. If we are going to allow into this country men who by breeding and inheritance are accustomed to take the law into their own hands, we must expect them to keep up these tactics when they get here."

Fault of Immigration System

Continuing further as an explanation to this statement the deputy commissioner had this to say: "The situation is this. The immigration laws do not keep the Black Handers out. These people are used to a very different legal system from ours. In Italy if a man commits a crime things go hard with him. Their laws differ from ours. Here they protect the rights of the individual. In Italy the laws are framed more for the protection of society. These fellows find that our laws do not hit them so vigorously as Italian laws. Therefore they come over here."

It was persistently rumored around police headquarters that Petrosino's mission to was not a voluntary one; that he went there much against his will. Deputy Police Commissioner Woods denied this vigorously.

"You can say as hard as you want to, officially, that Petrosino was very enthusiastic and hot on the job," said Mr. Woods, when asked about this rumor.

Detective Pelosino Black Hand Victim

Deputy Commissioner Woods wouldn't say whether Petrosino was unaccompanied.

There was a report yesterday that Petrosino's trip was not alone on business in connection with the New York Police Department, but that he was also in the service of the government to arrange a readjustment of the immigration laws.

Order Arrest of Black Handers

Upon the receipt of the news Inspector McCafferty, at the head of the detective bureau, took steps to find out if the assassination was the result of a plot formed in this country. He ordered his men to arrest any Italian suspected of being a member of the Black Hand. Telegrams were also sent to heads of police departments in all of the large cities, asking that Black-Handers be arrested.

When the Board of Aldermen refused to give Commissioner Bingham money to maintain a secret service squad, three wealthy men came to the front. Petrosino was placed at the head of the squad. There was information in Italy that was needed to get at the root of the Black Hand evil, and Petrosino was the man that General Bingham knew would succeed if anyone could, and he was sent abroad three months ago.

At headquarters one of the detectives said yesterday: "None of us knew where Joe was going when he went away, but we could see, although he was a policeman first, last and all the time, that he had a premonition that he would never return. He remarked before he went that he feared he would never return to his wife and child, but in his grim way smiled as he said it. He had many enemies and was constantly in fear of his life, but it never interfered with his work. Why, I know that when he went home nights he never entered his hallway until he first flashed a pocket light in every corner. I don't doubt in the least that Joe Petrosino was framed over there in Italy, and if a real investigation is ever made there will be developments that will be of a startling nature. It may be that he was followed when he went abroad, but then again no one knew that he was going away, and no one knew positively that he was there, unless he was betrayed by those in that country that he took into his confidence. Petrosino was too dangerous a man for the Italian criminals to allow to live. They threatened many times to get him and they kept their word."

Reporting: Immigrants 1803-1931

To Inspector McCafferty, head of the detective bureau, the news of the shooting of Petrosino was a great blow. McCafferty has worked with Petrosino, side by side, for many years, and when the detectives lined up yesterday morning they found McCafferty grim and determined. McCafferty paid a tribute to Petrosino for the great work he had done.

Los Angeles Herald
June 22, 1909

Chinese Slayer Eludes Officers

Murderer Of Elsie Sigel Is Yet At Large

Two Orientals Arrested, But Afford Little Data

Former Occupant of Room Where Girl Met Death Captured at Amsterdam, N. Y.

Restaurant Keeper Surrenders

New York, June 21.—After a bit of police flurry today, an hour or two of unverified report and telephoning between cities, the murder of Elsie Sigel resolved itself into an unsolved crime again tonight.

Chun Sin, who formerly occupied a room adjoining that where the girl's body was found, is held by the police at the up-state village of Amsterdam, N. Y., but what has been learned from him has cleared up the case but little.

At Schenectady the Chinese arrested today, at first thought to be Leon Ling or William L. Leon, who is sought as the girl's murderer, pretty well established that he is an unoffending Celestial who formerly worked in a New York restaurant and whose arrest was brought about merely through a striking resemblance to Leon Ling.

Chinese Slayer Eludes Officers

Tells Nothing of Value

The disappearance of Chun Sin about the time the murder was committed made the police eager for his apprehension, which was considered second in importance to that of Leon, but the interview with him at Amsterdam seems to have brought out nothing of value.

He maintains that he rarely associated with Leon, and, while acquainted with Elsie Sigel, knows nothing of the murder.

While the authorities upstate were putting two Chinese through an inquisition Sun Leong, keeper of the restaurant above which the body of the girl was found, was being questioned at police headquarters.

Sun Leong disappeared on the night the body was found, but quietly surrendered himself early today.

He is being detained as a material witness, but his voluntary surrender is taken to mean that he is not implicated in the crime.

In the midst of all the police activity the body of Elsie Sigel was quietly buried in Woodlawn cemetery.

Publicity Avoided

As the father had announced last night that he wished to avoid any more publicity, the coffin containing the mutilated form was taken directly from the morgue to the burying ground in a plain undertaking wagon.

The ceremony at the grave was strictly private and was attended only by her father, two brothers—Reginald and Theodore—and by her uncle, Franz Sigel.

Although the mission in Chinatown where Elsie Sigel formerly taught has been closed a meeting of Chinese who have been converted to Christianity was held in a Doyer street mission this afternoon to discuss plans for raising a fund to be offered as a reward for the capture of Elsie's slayer. A committee will go through Chinatown, soliciting subscriptions.

Fungy Mow's Statement

Rev. Fungy Mow, who acted as chairman, said Leon Ling had never been connected with the mission in any way and as far as he knew had never attended any school in Chinatown. Miss Sigel, he said, had taught Leon.

Theories as to the motive for the murder all center on the jealousy of Leon Ling. That he killed her because of her apparent friendship for Chu Gain, who is still detained as a material witness, is the predominating belief.

In support of this, Mrs. Florence Todd, one of the most prominent women workers in Chinatown, who knew Elsie Sigel and her mother intimately, said this afternoon:

"I know very well Chu Gain, who is under arrest. He is one of the few Chinese whom I would trust with my life. Mrs. Sigel and Elsie also knew him for many years. They were introduced to him through an uncle of his.

"I believe Elsie was in love with Chu Gain and would have married him, but that he would not marry her."

Here Mrs. Todd went into the most significant part of her statement—that bearing on Leon Ling. She said:

Mrs. Todd's Opinion

"Within the last year, despite her love for Chu Gain, Elsie became apparently infatuated with Leon Ling. But I think it was only a flirtation.

"He, I know, asked her to marry him, but she refused him. In fact she told me she refused him. Her mother knew all about it."

Despite her statement Mrs. Todd said she was not inclined to believe that Leon committed the murder, and she went on to relate that she has had a dream that Elsie Sigel had committed suicide.

Chu Gain, she said, came to her on the morning of June 14, five days after the murder is supposed to have been committed, and told her that he, too, had had a dream. In this dream Chu Gain, according to Mrs. Todd, had seen the form of the girl appear before him crying, "Chu, save me."

This seemed to worry the Chinese greatly because Elsie was missing at the time.

Called at House

The fact that Leon Ling called at the Sigel home Tuesday, June 8, the day before Miss Sigel's disappearance, and threatened to kill Chu Gain unless Elsie "stopped going with him" was made known today by Paul Sigel, the father of the murdered girl.

Mr. Sigel said also he believed Elsie was induced to visit Leon's room under the representation that Leon was ill: that she was killed on the day she left her home and that she did not go to Washington. Mr. Sigel said Leon was under the influence of liquor when he called.

In the love letters of Elsie Sigel to two Chinese is found the motive for the gruesome murder of Gen. Franz Sigel's granddaughter.

The night the body was discovered wedged into the old trunk of Leon Ling in English avenue the police found a score or more of letters which the girl had addressed to them.

They were endearing in tone and indicated a friendship more than platonic.

Find Two Hundred Letters

In searching Chinatown last night the detectives raided the private rooms of Chu Gain, owner of the famous Port Arthur Chinese restaurant, and there they found about 200 letters which had been addressed to him by Elsie Sigel.

These letters were even more endearing in tone than those found in Leon Ling's room. In these she addressed him as "My Own Dearest Beloved," "My Own Dear Chu." And she frequently signed herself "Ever Your Loving Elsie."

The Chu Gain letters gave the first information as to the motive of the murder. Miss Sigel told Chu Gain in some of these letters of her conduct with Leon Ling, told him not to be jealous and explained her object in maintaining her friendship for Ling.

The police will not give out the full contents of these letters. It is now supposed that Leon Ling decided to tragically end the romance of the girl he loved and his rival. Her affection for Chu Gain was known, as is shown by the letters received by Chu Gain, in which he and the girl are threatened with death unless their relations ceased.

Threat Executed

The murder apparently was the execution of that threat.

The Chinatown mission, popularly known as the "Girls' recreation rooms," was closed last night for the first time since it was opened eight years ago.

No explanation was given for this action, but it was supposed the murder of Elsie Sigel was responsible. It was in these rooms that Miss Sigel first undertook missionary work in Chinatown, and it was here that she was brought in contact with many of the residents of that section.

The young girl missionaries of Chinatown, like Elsie Sigel, use these rooms in which to meet the unfortunate women of Chinatown and there talk religion with them. On stated occasions Chinese were invited to the rooms and there they met the young girl missionaries.

In that manner many Chinese were induced to attend Christian Sunday schools in different parts of the city and from these first meetings many romances have developed, the Chinese marrying white women. The first of these weddings, which occurred eight years ago, created much comment, but recently there have been so many such alliances that little attention is paid to them.

Telegrams Confusing

Telegrams from various cities of the country relative to the supposed movements of Leon Ling and his missing roommate, Chong Sing, have only served to confuse the police in their search for the man wanted.

But the information from Chicago that two such men passed through there en route to Vancouver, B.C., is considered of importance and points west of Chicago have been notified to be on the lookout for them.

Leon Ling is reported to have been in Washington last Wednesday and Thursday, in company with his roommate, Chung Sing, and a white woman whose identity is not known.

The woman, it is said, lodged two nights with a family in C street, northwest, near Third street, and left there last Thursday night at 7 o'clock in company with two Chinese.

Members of the family at Washington today identified photographs of Leon Ling and Chung Sing as likenesses of the men who called on her. Occupants of the house declared the woman had said she was a trained nurse and was going to Baltimore to attend a patient.

She remained at the house from Wednesday afternoon until the two Chinese called for her Thursday night, without giving any reason for not hurrying to the patient.

The woman who rented the room declared the visitor was pale and much excited.

The Daily Democrat (Anadarko, OK)
September 27, 1909

The Black Hand Scourge

by Gerald A. Roderick

The assassination of Lieut. Joseph Petrosino in the streets of Palermo came very near to establishing the so-called "Black Hand" society in the minds of Americans as a definite organization such as the Sicilian Mafia and the Neapolitan Camorra. It was easy and alluring to argue that Petrosino, cleverest trailer of Italian crime and criminals, had fallen a victim to the international order of La Mano Nera. Writers were not lacking to invent details. His death had been decreed, they said, by one of the New York chapters of the Black Hand and the sentence executed by the home branch at Palermo.

"We almost believe that there is a Black Hand organization in Italy and America," said the editor of one of the big Italian dailies the day after the detective was shot down. "Until the death of Petrosino I never believed that there was head or tail to the bomb-throwing blackmailers, but the shot that struck Petrosino would seem to prove that there is a system behind them."

To one who remembered how violently that same editor had for years protested in Italian and in English that there was no such thing as a Black Hand society, the admission was surprising. Detectives of the

Manhattan and Brooklyn Italian police squads, who had always scoffed at an organized Black Hand, wondered if they had been mistaken. They searched the various quarters again for some trace of a central body, for some sign that there were directing officers. This Petrosino tragedy certainly savored of the dread Mafia and Camorra and there was not one of the lieutenant's squad who would not have gladly risked his life to lay hands on a real Black Hand chief.

Sober second thought and continued investigation, however, return the Black Hand to its proper category. It is not and never has been a society. It knows no chieftain, no scale of spoil division, no sacred oath. It has no meeting places, consequently holds no meetings. It is, in short, but a name for a brand of crime peculiar to Italian crooks, and it is so surprisingly successful because of the temperament of its south Italian victims and their inborn dread of the extortionist.

It is almost ludicrous to realize how the name that is now a world terror was invented. Some years ago the story of an Italian murder was running in the New York newspapers. The police made little headway and developments lagged. A space-writer on a certain morning paper needed more money than the story was bringing him. He could get more space only by giving a new twist to the crime, by working up an exclusive angle.

The victim of this murder had received a letter warning him that death would follow his failure to contribute a specified sum by a certain date. At the top of the sheet was a crude drawing of a fist holding a long, wicked-looking dagger. It was drawn with black ink, a somber, sinister emblem. For the reporter it held an idea. The name "Black Hand" leaped from his imagination, and there you are. With great circumstantial detail and flaring heads he introduced his find to the public. The murdered Italian was the victim of a rapacious organization of cut-throats. It was the American edition of the much-feared Mafia, a reincarnation of the deadly Camorra, and in it the reporter combined the worst features of each.

This characterization was an instantaneous hit. The murder story was again good for columns of space. The inventive reporter's rivals went him several better in succeeding editions. They found meeting places of the Black Hand. They traced other unsolved crimes of the Italian district to the same mythical source. The police said nothing. They had been unable to solve the crime, but if it was the work of a powerful secret organization there was some excuse for them.

The Black Hand Scourge

To the Italian blackmailers who then, as now, lived off the tribute they could wring from their brothers who worked or who had prospered in business, the appellation was a new and unexpected weapon, a stock in trade beyond value. It was not copyrighted and each and every one of them was free to use it. All "Little Italy" was talking of the Black Hand. Its translation into Italian—La Mano Nera—had an even more sinister sound. The next lot of blackmailing letters sent out bore the usual dagger, the skull and cross-bones, the bloody fingerprint, perhaps the long, black coffin, and every one was signed "La Mano Nera." The Black Hand was launched and the crimes since committed in its name number tens of thousands, the spoils collected have sent many a criminal back to Italy with a fortune according to the Sicilian rating, and not even the police will venture to estimate its cost in human life.

The Black Hand crimes all follow the same general lines, but that is no argument that there is an organized society. The yeggmen who terrorize country postmasters all work after an identical fashion, but no one has ever intimated that they were organized. Safecrackers the country over use the same tools and methods, but who has suspected them of holding conventions? The East Side gangs—the "Humpty" Jacksons, the Paul Kellys and the like—plunder similarly with more or less success, but the only connection between gang and gang is an occasional feud, the resulting "shooting up" of which gives the police opportunity to send a gangster or two to Sing Sing.

No Italian is too lonely or too poor to embark as a Black Hander. A sheet of paper, pen and ink, and enough knowledge of Italian to scrawl a few lines of demand and the accompanying threat are all that is necessary. Possible victims are on every hand. The barber in the dingy basement half-way down the block; the fat and timid grocery keeper on the corner; Antonio, of the tenement just below, who goes out early each morning all dressed in white to boss his gang of street sweepers—all these are possible victims of the single-handed Black Hander, and all sooner or later pay their tribute. Of course he signs himself "La Mano Nera," and then sits back to wait the working of the spell of temperamental dread.

About a table in a dingy, low-ceilinged basement wine shop off Mulberry Bend or over on Bleecker street four or five greasy, low-browed men gather of an afternoon over a bottle of cheap red wine. They puff at short-stemmed pipes or draw through straws on stogy-like Italian cigars that retail for half a cent. They are out of work and have been for weeks, perhaps, but it is not possible opportunities for labor that they discuss. Their need of money is mentioned quite frankly. In the next breath one of the gang recalls that Giuseppi, the tailor, looked sleek and prosperous standing in front of his shop an hour before. Another cries for pen and paper, which the master of the wineshop brings with never a smile, though he knows only too well the nature of the note that is about to be written. One is silently nominated to scrawl the command, another puts on the decorations and a third signs "La Mano Nera." The tailor is ordered to come three nights later at 7:30 o'clock to the stone arch in Washington Square and hand $200 to a little man with a hump on his back who will be waiting there. He is told further that if he fails or mentions the letter to the police death and destruction will be upon him.

The next morning Giuseppi has hardly opened his shop before the postman comes with the letter. One glance at the clumsily drawn black hand and the daggers scattered about is enough to tell him that the curse has fallen. For a time he is too frightened to read the sum of the extortion. The patrolman on beat passes his door, a broad-shouldered, strong-armed sign of law and order. A great temptation comes to Giuseppi. He will be brave as the American papers advise. He will call the police. He rushes out after the policeman, only to be overcome with a blue funk before he can blurt out his troubles, and ends by asking some foolish question that has no bearing on the terrifying letter. So on the appointed night he goes to Washington Square. The hunchback is there, waiting, with a particular eye for possible treachery from plainclothes policemen. Giuseppi slips the deformed one an envelope and both hurry from the spot in opposite directions. Around the next corner the hunchback becomes a changed man. The hump on his back disappears and the breaking off a bit of putty straightens a seemingly twisted nose. At the wine-shop the two hundred, perhaps the bulk of the tailor's savings, is speedily divided and the blackmailers are ready for other weeks of idleness. Again the Black Hand!

There is a possibility of big rewards in the games of plunder that has attracted criminals of skill, daring and brains. Many of them are ex-convicts from Italy, who plundered there in the name of the Mafia or the Camorra. Others are equally desperate criminals who got away from Italy before being caught and given the convict brand, which makes entry

The Black Hand Scourge

into America difficult and remaining here uncertain with Petrosino's band continually "fanning" the Italian quarters.

One of these skilled laborers of crime—or perhaps a pair of them—will gather about him four or five dull, unimaginative, lazy fellows—preferably "black sheep" of the town or section in Sicily from which the leader came—and there you have as near an organization as the Black Hand has yet perfected. This leader is known to his followers as a bad man. He has a record for speedy carving with a dagger, perhaps, or a much-to-be-envied knack of using his revolver quickly. He rules the gang by fear of bloody violence and does not even bother to extract oaths from them.

Italian bankers, contractors, wholesale dealers in spaghetti or olive oil or wine, owners of equities in mortgaged tenement houses—these are the victims of the big Black Handers. One thousand dollars is the least they strike for. Failure to pay means that a bomb of crude but deadly construction will be dropped in front of the marked man's bank, store or tenement house. Generally the bomb is so thoroughly overloaded with dynamite that it wrecks much surrounding property, but for that these land pirates care not. Often the innocent are slaughtered, but that brings not even a shrug from these hyenas of the tenements.

Every so-called Black Hand outrage helps on the game of plunder and adds to the fear of the mythical society. A lull in Black Hand outrages by no means indicates the inactivity of the plunderers. Generally it spells their continued success.

"You must always keep in mind," said Petrosino, the Palermo sacrifice to this sort of Italian crime, "that the commission of crimes of violence is not the main issue with this scum of the earth. If a man meets their demands, pays over their price, they are well satisfied to let him alone.

"Have you ever noticed," he continued "that there is more bomb throwing, more kidnapping, more mysterious murders in the winter months than in the spring, summer or early fall? The winter is the hard time of the year with all Italians and naturally the collections come harder. Men who have given up a few dollars now and then for months suddenly decide that, come what may, they will pay no more. According to the laws of the 'trade' this means punishment and there you have your outrages."

The intense love which a respectable Italian bears for his children has made kidnapping highly lucrative.

The Italian kidnapers about New York have been almost uniformly successful since they began signing their letters "La Mano Nera." In every case the child has been eventually returned to his home or left where the police would be sure to find him. Equally in every case there have been indications that the father, in spite of the most strict instructions to the contrary from the police, quietly paid over the amount demanded by the Black Handers or at least a satisfying portion of it.

Knowledge of kidnapping cases nearly always gets to the police and without delay. An Italian mother whose son fails to return from an errand to the bake shop around the corner or whose daughter disappears between the public school and her home does not fear even the Black Hand. Her husband may cringe and tremble when she suggests the police, but if he delays, the mother, with many wails of anguish, rushes to the nearest police station and blurts out the whole story. As a rule the police have little or nothing on which to work. They have the Black Hand letter demanding the ransom, but of what good is that when the leader of the gang may be that dapper, swarthy brother-in-law who is even then in the parlor mingling his temperamental tears with those of the family?

New York Sun
November 24, 1919

Reds Rush Here from Mexico

100 Russian Radicals Cross Over Line Daily, Congress Probers Find

Many More Are on Way

Revolution Schools Operating in New York— Sixteen Arrests in Cortland

Members of the House Committee on Immigration, who are here to investigate the faults and fallings of the present system of handling aliens, said last night that undesirable radicals are being smuggled into this country from Mexico at the rate of 100 a day, and that there is every reason to believe the Russian Bolsheviki have laid plans to flood this country with propagandists as soon as they can arrange an armistice with their enemies and a lifting of the blockade. Representative Albert Johnson of Washington, chairman of the committee, said he had been informed that Yokohama, Tokyo and other Asiatic cities are filled with Russian reds awaiting an opportunity to enter the United States and that large groups in Switzerland are also planning an early invasion. "Though far scattered," he said, "there is every evidence that these 'reds' are all part of a well organized system.

"They aim at establishing themselves here," he added, "for two reasons. They feel that our generally lenient laws will enable them to work with little interference and they regard our enormous alien population as a fertile field in which to disseminate their propaganda." Mr. Johnson said that the Congress committee had discovered that at present numerous "red" schools in this city are teaching violent revolutionary doctrines to newly landed immigrants. "Many foreigners," he charged, "come here with minds free from such ideas and are soiled upon by propagandists of various "red" groups who induce them to visit their organizations, where every effort is made to convert them into dangerous Bolsheviki."

Seek Arrest to Save Carfare

In connection with their discovery at a hearing on Ellis Island on Saturday that anarchists and Bolsheviki seized for deportation in various parts of the country are turned loose after their arrival in New York the members of the committee said that they had learned also that many "reds" seek arrest on deportation warrants simply to obtain free transportation to New York.

"When arrested in Western cities," Representative Johnson said, "these radicals frequently put up no defense. After being brought to New York at the expense of the federal government they produce evidence to show that they are American citizens and the authorities are obliged to release them here."

The representative expressed interest in the fact that the Department of Labor never has regarded membership in the I. W. W. as ground for deportation, and that it has been no bar to obtaining American citizenship here.

The committee will continue their investigations on Ellis Island today, going particularly into the cases of the anarchists and Bolsheviki rounded up recently and of the trainload of "reds" brought here last spring, only to be loosed upon the New York public.

The members have been informed that influence frequently has been exerted by powerful law firms here to free dangerous radicals and that attorneys in close touch with official Washington have been retained by "reds" with results satisfactory to their clients and disastrous to public welfare. These charges and a multitude of others will be looked into and the committee will endeavor to fix the blame.

Yesterday the entire committee, consisting of representatives Johnson, Rader, Siegel, Vaile, Baker, Swops, Welty, Box and Wilson, accompanied officials of the Department of Immigration aboard the Adriatic to gain firsthand knowledge of the manner in which the aliens are handled on entering this port. A few hours' observation sufficed to convince them that the present machinery is inadequate. They found that one examiner was supposed to do the work of two, and that the force was unable to comply literally with the terms of the immigration laws.

Reds Rush Here from Mexico

Sweeping Inquiry Planned

It was intimated that their investigation may include a complete overhauling of the records of the administration of the local bureau by Frederick C Howe, although the committee men asserted that they are not directing their inquiry at any one man or department.

Chairman Johnson expressed the opinion that the head of the Ellis Island bureau had been vested with entirely too much authority, asserting that although this official is technically supposed to be subordinate to the commissioner-general in Washington, he frequently has been able to go over the commissioner-general's head on important matters, and is drawing larger pay than his superior. This is because the head of the local bureau receives $1,800 a year extra for taking charge of alien property.

Today's inquiry will begin at 10 A.M., and many inspectors and inmates of the island will be examined. The committee's discovery regarding the careless release of "reds" by immigration authorities here dovetails with charges made by Alexander I. Rorke, assistant district attorney in charge of the prosecution of many Bolsheviki. Mr. Rorke said that in innumerable cases violent radicals turned over to the federal authorities for deportation have been arrested a few weeks later in police raids. The district attorney's office, he said, has frequently been surprised to discover in their prisoners persons whom they thought safe and sound behind federal bars.

When Mr. Rorke continues his inquiry today into the affairs of the Communist party he will call as his principal witness Mrs. Rose Pastor Stokes, who was questioned a few minutes at Friday's session of the extraordinary grand jury.

Since Saturday reports have reached the police that Communists and other violent radicals have been endeavoring to tamper with grand jury witnesses. Certain persons called to testify in the inquiry now under way are said to have been waited on by delegations of Communists who have taken them to uptown restaurants for secret conference. One witness subpoenaed was seen Friday night in Broadway cafe, conferring with a group of the persons against whom the inquiry is directed. This conference was held within a few hours after that witness had been ordered to appear for examination.

16 Russians Taken at Cortland

Sixteen Russians charged with circulating seditious literature were arrested yesterday at a meeting in Cortland, N.Y., the home city of Senator Clayton E. Lusk, chairman of the Lesgislative Committee on Bolshevism. They were seized at a meeting.

Members of the American Legion in New York state have been asked by Russell E. Sard, state commander, to join in an intensive war upon Bolshevism, I.W.W.ism and other forms of defiance of law and order. In instructions sent to all of the 765 posts of this state the members are requested to cooperate in detecting anti-American activities and to show dangerous radicals that New York state is a bad place for them in which to remain.

Together with these instructions there was sent to every post a copy of a telegram received at the local headquarters, 149 Nassau Street, from Grand Hodge Post, No. 17, of Centralia, Wash., of which the servicemen recently slain by the I.W.W. were members. This telegram reads:

"Four of our comrades murdered by I.W.W. Grant Hodge Post, No. 17, demands immediate action by every American Legion post for congressional action on individuals and organizations in America and a national publicity campaign to carry on Americanism. Line up your local posts and state organization of the legion. Congress convenes December 1st. Americanism must be the big issue. A publicity campaign carried on by every post for the next ten days will win our battle. Act today. Get this to every press in your state and before every post for immediate action. A copy of this telegram goes to every state secretary and to national headquarters of the American Legion."

The New York State Department of the American Legion has wired that it will back the Centralia men to the limit on the Americanization issue.

The Brainerd Daily Dispatch (Brainerd, MN)
December 21, 1919

3 Hundred Reds Sail for Russia

Taken from New York on Transport Buford on Sunday

New York, Dec. 21—The United States army transport Buford, ark of the Soviet, sailed before dawn today with a cargo of anarchists, communists, and radicals banned from America for conspiring against its government. The ship's destination was hidden in sealed orders, but the 249 passengers expected to be landed at some far northern port giving access to Soviet Russia.

"Long live the revolution in America!" was chanted defiantly by the motley crowd on the decks of the steel gray troop ship as she churned her way past the Statue of Liberty. Now and then they cursed in chorus at the United States and the men who had cut short their propaganda here. Not until the Buford steamed out of the Narrows between forts Hamilton and Wadsworth did the din cease. Over their heads whipping in the wind the Stars and Stripes floated from the masthead.

Destination Still a Secret

The autocrats of all the Russians of the transport were Alexander Berkman and Emma Goldman, his companion for 30 years. With them were 245 men and two women—Ethel Bernstein and Dora Lipkin. None knew where they would debark and even Capt. C.A. Hitchcock, commander of the veteran transport, was no better off.

At daybreak tomorrow Colonel Hilton, commanding the troops on board as guard, will hand the skipper his instructions. Only a few high officials of the war and labor departments know the ship's destination. The voyage will last 18 days unless it is prolonged by unfavorable weather. The presumption is that the Buford will land at Hanme, Helsingfors or Abo in Finland, which are connected by rail with Bielo-Osporoff on the Russian frontier. It was intimated in official quarters that arrangements have been made with the Finnish government to permit the passage of the Russians through that country.

The transfer from Ellis Island to the Buford of the agitators who have preached death and destruction was an event unique in the annals of this nation. Seized in raids in all parts of the country, they were mobilized here for deportation. An elaborate screen of secrecy was thrown about the preparations for sending them away.

Set Forth in Darkness

It was in the darkest hours of the night that an army tug drew up at the dock of the immigration station to take aboard the undesirables for the 7 mile journey down the bay to the Buford. Two dozen soldiers armed with rifles and as many immigration inspectors carrying night sticks patrolled the shores of Ellis Island until the tug arrived at 5:15 a.m. The Reds were marched single file between two lines of guard from the immigration barracks to the boat landing, each carrying baggage. A score of agents of the Department of Justice circulated among the Russians waiting to begin their journey. These agents and the soldiers guards on the island went on board the tug with the deportees and took them to the transport.

A revenue cutter and two other army tugs formed an escort for the Reds and one tug lay alongside while they were being transferred to the Buford to prevent attempts by those reluctant to leave to swim the half mile to the short of Staten Island.

While all the anarchists had professed joy at the thought of returning to Russia, a few of them wept and most of them seemed downcast as they stepped on board the tug for the grim journey through the darkness of the harbor to the troop ship.

New York Tribune
April 4, 1920

How Shall the Alien Be Made Into a Good American?

Not by Means of Persecution and Repressive Legislation, Says Frances A. Kellor

Foreigners Who Really Want to Become Good Citizens Are Confused by Conflicting Rules

by Frances A. Kellor

It would be amusing were it not so pathetic to see the attacks and counter attacks on Americanization. Many persons in the stress of the war started out to Americanize the alien. Then someone suggested that the Americans be Americanized and from that developed the "Americanization of the navy," "Americanization of the treaty," and every conceivable project that could be loaded on the popular bandwagon has been labeled Americanization. We have now reached the stage where the chairman of the California Commission on Housing and Immigration writes an article on the "Menace of Americanization."

Americanization is perhaps the best present-day illustration of the fallacy of the campaign method of activity and of the high pressure methods used to obtain results in this country. We have just held a Loyalty Week, shaking hands with everyone and then forgetting that we have met him or where he lives. We invite immigrants into membership in our patriotic organizations and then forget them until their dues are payable again. We call them "Mike" during a drive of some kind or another and do not know them in their store clothes on Sunday.

Two Movements

There are two nationwide movements in America and many of our good citizens are in both. One is Americanization, as shown by the holding of Loyalty Week, the registration of fire underwriters to conduct local work, the establishment of an Americanization division of the American Legion, the installation of Americanization lecture courses in our colleges, the activities of hundreds of religious and social service groups, and the schoolhouse activities of an increasing number of public school superintendents.

The other is the antagonism to the immigrant expressed in proposed public legislation that will increase many-fold the difficulties of aliens living in America. These are both state and federal. "To deport and expel" is one of the commonest phrases in such bills. If all the proposed laws were passed there would not be enough ships for deportations and voluntary departures. One man estimates that it would take 10,000 Bufords and with our present shipping facilities a period of more than five years. Incidentally, it would deprive the country of half of its unskilled labor.

When immigrants want to go back to their homelands they must go through almost endless formalities in obtaining permits and visas of passports. When they want to come to America they must pay a poll tax in this country of $8. Now comes an administration measure to charge a fee of $9 for each visa of the passport and $1 for each application for a visa, the fees to be collected by the American consulate at the port where the immigrant embarks for this country.

Means a Large Sum

Thus it is proposed to make the immigrant pay $18 in fees to the United States government. For some of the races on which America depends for labor this means a large sum of money at the present rate of exchange. The Polish and old Austro-Hungarian peoples would have to pay 4,500 kronen, or nearly twenty times as much as the immigrant used to pay for his passage to the United States before the war.

If to that amount be added the transportation fees charged at the present time the immigrant from Poland or Lithuania or the Baltic provinces would have to pay between 80,000 to 100,000 kronen, or the equivalent of $833 today. For this amount of money a man can buy a home or a farm in Poland or other countries of Europe.

What is the immigrant to think who in the morning is invited to learn English and become a citizen and in the evening newspaper is called

How Shall the Alien Be Made Into a Good American?

a "Red" and told to get back home; who in the morning is asked to take out his first papers and in the evening learns that citizenship means nothing to him in his home country; who at 9 a.m. is urged to join the night school and at 9 p. m. finds the teacher who does not know how to teach him. One day he is told by the United States government that as an alien he can be exempt from military service, even as Americans are exempt in countries overseas, and on another day he sees a number of bills introduced by Congressmen to deport and punish him for availing himself of his rights. One day he is told he cannot bring his sister to America because she is illiterate and the next he reads of thousands of Mexicans who are allowed to enter by a special law in their favor.

A Case of Indigestion

America certainly has indigestion, and it has not made a diagnosis nor found the remedy. There are 15,000,000 foreign-born people and 42,000 local societies of the foreign born and thousands of colonies east of the Mississippi River. These and 5,000 private immigrant banks and 1,500 foreign-language newspapers are thinking and talking in forty-two different dialects and acting according to the customs and traditions and lights of countries about which Americans know little or nothing. No wonder that the Americanization doctors who set out with their pill boxes and their prescriptions for learning English and for hurrying up citizenship and their patent medicines of mass meetings for loyalty and the high-pressure feeding process of Americanism are now wondering what is the matter with Americanization. No superficial remedies will cure a disease so long neglected, revealing causes centuries old and imported from all of the countries of the world.

Of course, the trouble is that so many think of foreignism as a disease and that it has to be cured and that men cannot be happy nor safe nor prosperous until it is. Doubtless the man who saw the first sunrise thought it was a menace and not a blessing, and the man who sees for the first time the immigrant in the mass, having avoided him individually all his life, thinks he is an unmixed evil. Americanization, whatever its ultimate fate, has awakened the native American and he is taking it rather seriously. It has also awakened the immigrant and he is also taking it seriously, for he is feeling the effect of deportations and repression. Both groups are in action, but to what end? Will the American be happy in repression? Will the immigrant be glad to go back home and say the vaunted freedom of America did not materialize?

This brings us down to fundamentals, namely, immigration and emigration. We have had both for many years. The wave of Americanization and the revival of Americanism seem not to have made a dent in the situation. Americans like the froth of education. In our campaigns we use moving pictures; we are fascinated by the mechanics of mass meetings and billboards and posters and pay envelope stickers. But the great questions are: What is being said at meetings? Do any two billboards or posters tell enough of the same story to convince an immigrant of what the truth is about America? The immigrant wants to know the simple and fundamental things about us. Where is the answer that can set his mind at rest and his heart at peace?

Must Be Treated White

He asks: "Do you want us in America or do you not?" A headline or a mass meeting or a poster is not the kind of answer he needs. Our attitude should be stated in our immigration laws of admission. Unless they are encouraged to bring over their families, unless they get work when they arrive and are treated "white" on the job and like men when they are off of it, they are not convinced. There is hardly a man of foreign birth who goes to an Americanization meeting that doesn't try to square what is said there with what happens to him day by day. Does it square? That is the only kind of answer he understands when he asks, "Do you want me or do you not; do you want all of us in America or only some of us, and which ones?" The probabilities are that nine-tenths of the Americanizers have not made up their minds.

Once admitted to America he again asks, "Do you want us to stay here or go back?" He says to us:

"We have money, but we would like to buy a home with a garden and a flower pot in the window in a nice neighborhood. Will the American stay or move out if we come in? We want to put our money in the banks and to buy bonds. We know it is safer than teapots and mattresses. But how the American banker scowls at us because we have to come in our dirty clothes! We work ten or twelve hours in the factory or mine and have

How Shall the Alien Be Made Into a Good American?

little time to change or clean up and we don't want to keep our money over Sunday. Do you want us to learn English? We hear a great deal about it, but we cannot find any classes or teachers that know how to teach or have any patience or who show us that it helps us to get on in America to learn the language."

What Does America Think?

What is the alien to think? What are we to think about immigration? Beyond opening the doors and letting the immigrant in and forgetting him until it is time to expel him, America is officially silent or chaotic in its idea of immigration. In general it is known what labor thinks and what capital thinks; what the restrictionist and anti-restrictionist think; what this hobbyist or that hobbyist thinks; what this or that society recommends. But what does America, officially and in its majority public opinion, think? Who speaks for America at home? Is it the Immigration Service, the Naturalization Bureau, the Bureau of Education, the passport division of the Treasury Department, the Attorney General's office, the Alien Property Custodian, or the raid and deportation squad, or the Post Office Department? If they all speak for America, what is the immigrant to think? If American officials charged with law enforcement differ so much, can the immigrant be expected to understand America?

If one happens to be an immigrant and desires to become a citizen and learn English and wants to bring over his family or send money home; if he wants to own a foreign language newspaper and to invest in America—and the immigrant may desire all these things—he is apt to hear from all of these departments in different ways, couched in language that is hard to understand without a lawyer, because most officials are too busy to explain it to him except by warrants and fines.

Every day or so a new bill is introduced in Congress which makes him more nervous than ever about democracy. One of the latest steps toward winning the foreign-born over to Americanism has been the introduction of a bill in the Senate to exclude foreign-language newspapers from second-class mailing privileges. This is by way of being reward for their loyalty during the war and as an appreciation of the fact that 99 per cent of the foreign-language newspapers have been loyal and have not tended in any way toward dangerous ultra-radicalism.

No two of these officials know what the other is saying or doing, and the immigrant cannot be helped by these officials because they do not know.

Preaching and Practice

The trouble with Americanization is that the distance between preaching and practice is so great that the alien cannot span it. Americans still regard it too much as a pastime when they approach it as citizen or as a "solemn duty" with a "weather eye" to political advantages. The outlook is hopeful, however, and increasingly men are seeding more fundamental methods.

Does America want the immigrant here? Let it say so in laws a definite, constructive, manly way instead of contenting ourselves with an instrument full of negatives and evasions and compromises.

Does America want the immigrant to become a citizen? Let it be about raising the standards and abolish the old dead wood of technicalities that impose hardships that have no value today in promoting citizenship.

Does America want him to stay here? Let it permit him to use his own language and go to his own meetings and realize his dream of freedom in America. Does America want him to learn English? Then let it provide classes and make it worth his while to learn English.

Does America want his savings invested in America? Then have the American banker realize his responsibility and secure his deposit and sell American investments to him.

Americans can well take some of the time spent in knocking Americanization and practice Americanism so that the immigrant will know what is required of him. It is a mistake to advertise putting on string of Bufords and then have the Commissioner General of Immigration announce that he is not sure they will sail, as the cost may be too high after his passengers are waiting and have paid their fares. This is poor business, either in the steamship business or in Americanism. It is the kind of thing the immigrant does not understand. America cannot afford to have him groping in the dark.

One of the reasons for the immigrant's not fitting better into American life is that America is a constantly shifting sand of ideas and activities into which he is afraid to root.

The Problem of Immigration

America Must Think First

What is the immigrant to think? America must do its own thinking first and tell the immigrant its conclusions and then talk them out with him. Then America will have a policy to proceed upon which will command the respect of the world and which will assimilate the alien. At present our immigration policy is nothing but an "admission exclusion" law that does not meet post-war conditions. We have a naturalization law that belongs to the Dark Ages and a public opinion that is a mass of conjecture, change and counter charges. It is no wonder that the immigrant finds it difficult to think straight about America when native Americans are in a mental morass themselves.

Wilmington Morning News
December 28, 1920

The Problem of Immigration

by Dr. Leopold Vaccaro

THE American-born children raised in the ghetto homes keeping boarders are under great moral and educational handicap, and were it not for the leveling influence of our public school, the second generation problem would be of a graver import. But the low standard of living is no fault of the immigrant. He is paying in some instances just as much rent as an American-born in a better section of the city. The slum, as well as these foreign communities, could be improved if the city took an active interest, but then comes the ward politics, and the community exploiter, who is usually a compatriot and who carries the foreign vote in his "vest pocket." The churches themselves in many instances fail to measure up to their responsibilities. Several would gladly foot any bill rather than receive foreigners into their fold. Some churches surrounded by foreign settlements were sold and the proceeds sent to the Board of Foreign Missions rather than swing the doors open to these newer citizens.

Reporting: Immigrants 1803-1931

Practically all the immigrants come from rural regions, where the disinfecting actinic rays of the sun and the oxidizing properties of the open air destroy the disease-producing germs. They are now huddled into dark, stenchy, unsanitary tenement houses or barns owned by respectable citizens or enriched immigrants. The real league of nations that all civic, political and philanthropic associations should help are these little ghettos in our cities. Certainly it is no credit to any community to allow such a condition of affairs. It is, however, true that as the economic position of the foreign community member improves, he changes his residence to a better location and his home, whether due to the laws of imitation or inherent love for cleaner environment, stands on a par with the native-born of the same social class. The standard of living of the adult second generation corresponds to that of the native of the older immigrants.

The second point is that immigration reduces wages. This objection is raised by labor organizations. Legislation against contract labor was the outcome of this agitation. The tendency of the immigrant is to work for some salary rather than nothing at all. His dependents at home would force him to any condition of labor or remuneration and his low standard of living would allow him to accept any pay. But the immigrants also have learned the art of strikes, as was determined by the Kenyon Committee last year investigating industrial troubles in western Pennsylvania; in fact, the tendency is now to blame the foreign element for every labor difficulty, and disregard the intellectual native labor leaders.

Every working man desires legitimate ascendency in the wage scale, and the immigrant who has left his country for economic reasons is no exception to this rule. He would like more pay if he could get it. If the native worker considers competition as it concerns him individually, he is right, but if he looks at the question from the angle of the general good to the nation, he is wrong; for the wealth produced by the immigrant is bound to reverberate on us all.

The fourth objection to immigration is that it increases criminality. This statement is not borne out by statistics; crimes have not increased in proportion to immigration but have changed in character. Whereas once offenses were chiefly against property, now they are against person. Homicides, assaults and battery are in the main confined to the members of a racial group and are the results of peculiar feelings of their own.

How the International Rogues Greet the Immigrants

The congestion of cities has made a real problem for America. The immigrant peasant of today has a particular love for the city; its many diversions fascinate him and detract him from the agricultural pursuits to which he is adapted. The immigrants from northwestern Europe sought the farms; they are now prosperous and have made splendid citizens. The late newcomers remain in the cities. The recent New York crime wave is associated by some persons with the presence of so many foreigners and their descendants. It is said that if the immigrant after landing goes to a western community he will return and settle in some large centre of the East. The manufacturing industries make his stay possible. The large presence of his compatriots, speaking his own language and living after the fashion of the old country, fastens him to the city. Congestion can be relieved by assigning to these immigrants lands in the West and South, as was done before the Civil War, but in that event a check might prove a stimulus; the population pressure would be removed and make room for another stream of immigrants, as the historic precedent teaches us. This phase of the problem is highly complicated. It may be that a strong Americanization crusade might solve it.

The arguments in favor of immigration are several. Perhaps the strongest is the industrial one. No industry can get along without foreign unskilled labor. At present none employs less than fifty percent. The world war, by automatically suspending immigration, has caused a shortage of manpower of over five million men.

New York Herald
April 30, 1922

How the International Rogues Greet the Immigrants

Gullible Newcomers Easy Prey for Well Organized Band Which Not Only Tricks Them Out of Their Own Savings But Gathers in the Little Fortunes of the Relatives Back Home

A surprising exposé of the operations of an international ring of swindlers who prey upon immigrants newly arrived in America has just been made by Harry H. Schlacht, formerly chairman of the United States Welfare Commission at Ellis Island and now president of the Downtown Chamber of Commerce, New York. Mr. Schlacht reveals the existence of a well-organized band of suave, debonair rogues who, with affiliations reaching into almost every country in Europe from which the more prosperous immigrants come, has succeeded within the last two years in filching many millions of dollars from ignorant newcomers to America.

Mr. Schlacht's information is built upon his term as Welfare Commissioner at Ellis Island, the landing place of all immigrants who come to this harbor. He describes in detail the most successful operation of the swindlers, and discloses that they seem to have unlimited financial backing and extreme cleverness in remaining narrowly within the law.

This, the most successful swindling plan, is conducted under the guise of "international banking." The tricksters are sufficiently familiar with human psychology to know that a banker may, in the minds of the usual immigrants, include a multitude of sins. The peasant and the workman traditionally stand in awe of the man who moves in the glamour of banking associations.

In New York there seems to be a little company of men who present themselves to the incoming immigrants as "international bankers." These men know that as a rule the immigrant coming to America leaves behind him a family, or at least close relatives, to whom he has promised that he will find a way to send for them. He has come believing more or less that money may be picked from bushes in the New World and that it will not be long before the wife, the mother and father, the sweetheart or the uncles and aunts may follow him. He promises faithfully to send the money "within just a little while."

He is not so greatly astonished, therefore, when immediately after his arrival, and before he has learned that the bushes that grow money for the passerby to pick are planted only at the top of high hills which are hard to reach, he is approached by a sleek, expensively dressed and prosperous looking "business man," who greets him with an astonishing familiarity with his name and the place of his origin and proposes a way that the family or the relatives may be brought to America at once.

The "business man," who introduces himself as a banker and who presents a neatly engraved calling card to prove his status, has found little difficulty in learning the name and former residence in Europe of the newly arrived immigrant. The records at Ellis Island gave him this information. Yet the immigrant himself is most deeply impressed by this knowledge and believes at once his caller's explanation that "his friends at home, who had learned of the banker's business in America, had written him asking him to call upon the newcomer here."

With this introduction properly staged and passed the "banker" makes an attractive proposition.

"My bank is sending to Italy," or Scandinavia, or Hungary, or France, or whatever country the immigrant has come from, "one of the members of our staff, who has been commissioned to arrange for transportation to America of the relatives of a number of your countrymen who have just arrived, like you, in New York.

"If you wish to have us undertake a similar mission for you we would be very glad to bring your father, or your mother, or your wife, or whomever you would like to have brought over, without further delay. It will not cost near as much as you anticipate if you make your arrangements at once, and we will be very glad to accept what little money you may have about you."

It is established that during the first weeks or months in America the immigrant who has come, quite often alone, is lonely for the associates he left behind. The dream of being able quickly to bring over parents, or relatives, or perhaps the wife who has promised to wait patiently until he could afford it, remains very vivid with him. He yearns for the encouragement and the accustomed society which the presence of those who were close to him at home would mean in this strange country. It is the psychological time for the broaching of any proposition which would seem to hurry the arrival of those whose presence here he most desires.

The average immigrant is as unsuspecting as a child. He has as a rule been brought up in an atmosphere of haggling, barter and trade. He has learned to fight and bargain for every necessity. Fundamentally he is shrewd and quite often clever. But in the atmosphere of the new country, surrounded by what to him is an imposing grandeur of great buildings, prosperous people who rush to and fro, apparently always bent upon important business, and with the signs of lavishness and luxury on every hand, his suspicions of his fellow man are as a rule in abeyance for quite some time. Even as he has accepted as a fact the almost unbelievable splendor of the great New World, so he is ready to accept as true whatever is told him by any of the New World's representatives. And to him who could be a more substantial representative of the opulence around him than a "great international banker"?

The majority of immigrants come to America with quite a little hoard of savings. They amount of course as a rule to only a few dollars measured in comparison with the average New World wealth. But they are at any rate dollars, and quite often the immigrant has brought with him two or three hundred of them. But even though he has but $50 left by the time the spurious banker reaches him, or even if he has made no new friends who will lend him more than this, the "banker" is quite satisfied.

He proposes that whatever amount it is the immigrant can produce be given to him. He promises that the "representative of his bank" will faithfully deliver the message to the relatives back home which the immigrant may give him to carry, and that he will see that whatever more money is necessary is advanced, and that the relatives—father, mother, sweetheart, or uncle or aunt—are duly brought back on the very next steamer.

Thus he procures from the unsuspecting, newly arrived immigrant a written or a verbal message to the folk at home. And of course becomes fully informed of the names, addresses and general station of these, who are waiting on the other side to be sent for by the one who came first.

Not long after a "representative" of the "banker" actually does sail for Europe. He carries with him not only the messages and the names and addresses furnished by the one immigrant mentioned above but has been similarly equipped by scores and scores of others. His sailing is a step toward the climax of a campaign extended over several weeks of preparation in this country, during which time hundreds of newly arrived immigrants have been approached by the members of the swindling band.

On the other side this representative of the rogues here one by one hunts out the relatives to whom he has been given letters and messages. Assuming that it is a mother and father, living perhaps out in the garden lands beyond Naples, whom the immigrant mentioned above wishes to have with him in America, the procedure of the representative who is visiting Italy would be:

Approaching the couple, whom he probably will find in a cottage set in the midst of a prosperous vegetable garden, he brings untold joy to them, when, hat and gloves in hand, he bows ceremoniously and announces that he has come—come especially to see them—as the agent of their Antonio, who has been so fortunate in America.

One may easily picture the awe and happiness with which Antonio's parents receive this distinguished looking visitor from the much-fabled America. He stands before them a spectacular symbol of the great company of rich and powerful friends whom their Antonio must already have gathered about him in the new land. They are almost pathetically joyous to learn that Antonio has longed for them more than even they expected. The mother's eyes, perhaps, will grow quite dim when the stranger tells her how anxiously her Antonio is waiting to greet her in America with his arms held open ready to enfold her.

And no doubt the dampness will become actual tears when the visitor says: "And so I have come to take you back with me to where your Antonio is waiting." He explains that it was just for them he has come to Italy, although, of course, while he is there, there are a few others whom he is taking back with him to their sons and husbands who went before. They will be company on the ship, he adds.

"Of course, there is a slight arrangement that will be necessary. Antonio has not yet been able to save a great amount of money, and what he has earned he has preferred to spend in the preparations of a beautiful little home for himself and his mother and father. He has furnished this home very prettily indeed and has already planted a garden and built a nice shed for the cow and quite a substantial pen for the pig. So this has taken nearly all of Antonio's money, but that is easily remedied.

"You see, Antonio knew that you could easily raise sufficient money here to pay the small expense of your transportation abroad—even by selling the cottage and the garden. And that would be quite all right, since at Antonio's home there will be no need to keep possession of this property over here."

If there is any hesitancy in the minds of the old father and mother it is quickly dissipated when the visitor refers them again to the letter which Antonio had given him to give them. Antonio had expressed in this letter his happiness at thus being able to make it possible for them to join him at once. Certainly he must have meant, just as the stranger said, for them to sell the home and raise what money they could in other ways and allow this kind friend of his to bring them on the ship that sails in just a few days.

And so the immigrant's father and mother sell the little plot of ground that has been in their family for many generations and turn the proceeds over to the representative of the "great New York bankers." They meet him a few days later at the pier, and he ushers them aboard with all the others whom he has victimized in the same way.

Instead of a "few" as company there are scores, all of whom have sold some valuable possession, homes or jewelry, or have taken the last of their savings to furnish the stranger the money which he has told them was required for their transportation and "a few other little expenses."

None of these is ill at ease. All have had messages from America, all have been assured that homes and prosperity were awaiting them in the new and magic land.

And so the representative of the "international bankers" brings them to Ellis Island. As he comes first class, he comes with the ship to its dock and leaves it to disappear in the city. In his pockets are from $100 to $200 for each of the relatives he has brought over, this amount being the "few extra expenses" which he had assured his victims would be incurred.

Often the Antonios over here do not even know that their relatives are arriving. They, as a rule, are not at Ellis Island to greet them. It is not infrequent that the new arrivals are returned to Europe. Such as do find the way to communicate with those whom they expected to meet them are sadly disillusioned when they are finally brought in and learn how they had been duped.

Usually the "international bankers" manage to keep within the law, or at least so surround themselves with circumstances that it is hard to convict them of the felonies they undoubtedly commit. They actually deliver the messages given them by the Antonios on this side. They actually make the trip across to the homes of the relatives abroad. They promise in return for the money raised for them on the other side nothing more than to bring the relatives to this country. Of course they ornament and elaborate this promise and decorate it with many glowing verbal pictures. But they do not put these decorations down on paper and do not commit themselves before witnesses, and at any rate the unfortunates just arriving in this country do not know the methods of making formal complaints.

This is just one of the swindling operations Mr. Schlacht has revealed. There are many others and there are many variations of this one. Foreign language newspapers are quite often used by the "international

Hardships Third Class Immigrants Have to Bear at Ellis Island

bankers" to advertise their sending abroad a representative to "bring to this country friends of those who already have arrived." Replies to these advertisements, in which newly arrived immigrants on this side are invited to communicate with the advertiser and to trust to him whatever letters they may wish to send home, are always heavy. From among these replies names and facts are gathered with which the "bankers" can line up their prospective victims.

Consistent effort has been made to stamp out this practice. Largely these efforts already have succeeded, although the swindlers still are active. As fast as one plan is thus disclosed and action taken to protect the immigrants from it, others are hatched and other schemes are worked out. Mr. Schlacht has made many recommendations for further protection of the immigrants and has enlisted the support of the Downtown Chamber of Commerce, which is now inaugurating a sturdy campaign for a more complete watchfulness over the safety and interests of all newly arrived immigrants.

The New York Times
December 17, 1922

Hardships Third Class Immigrants Have to Bear At Ellis Island

Quotas Cause Crowding

Rush First of Month Jams Quarters to the Limit

Davis Proposes Changes

But British Officials Suggested Plan of Segregation Would Itself Work Injustice

Hugh McNiel, Under Secretary of Foreign Affairs and a responsible spokesman for the British government, has recently criticized our treatment of immigrants. Our first reaction is to resent this interference in

America's domestic policy, then we remember that our own Teddy Roosevelt told England how she ought to manage Egypt. We do, however, want to know whether his criticism is just. With this end in view the writer has investigated the subject thoroughly, has talked with Secretary Davis and Commissioner Husband and, through the courtesy of Robert Todd, head of the local immigration station, inspected Ellis Island and was permitted to talk to a large number of the immigrants themselves.

The scope of this article will be limited to the reception and handling of the immigrant. The wisdom of the immigration law will not be discussed; save in so far as is necessary to explain some of the restrictions and the reason for some of the inconveniences borne by the immigrant.

Mr. McNiel's principal objection to the American immigration system is based largely upon its failure to make any distinction between the educated yeomanry of Anglo-Saxon blood, who are already more or less accustomed to American standards, and the riffraff of Europe, who will in future be known by numbers on the payroll of American industry. This criticism is manifestly unjust. Who is to have the despotic power to determine whether an individual is of the better class? What administration would feel willing to label the citizens of a friendly power as belonging to an inferior race? If such discrimination were expedient it would often work an injustice even if administered with honest intention. Inability to speak our language would place a newcomer at a disadvantage before the new autocrats in the immigration service, which Mr. McNiel would have us establish. The foreigner unaccustomed to our language, dressed in his native costume, ignorant of our social customs, would have a poor chance to be registered as a Class A immigrant and therefore be entitled to superior consideration, though he might be well educated in his own tongue and as efficient and intelligent as his more fortunate fellow-immigrant. It can thus be seen that it is impractical to rate immigrants by an arbitrary decision of the Immigration Bureau in Washington through the establishment of favored nations or to leave it to the local officials to determine the class of the individual immigrant.

The only discrimination that can be justly applied is based on the class in which the immigrant comes to America. First-class passengers, from whatever country, are not forced to go to Ellis Island and are not detained there unless in a particular case there is some specific reason for America's refusal to admit. Second-class passengers also have certain privileges. The third-class passengers are under closer scrutiny and subject to more restrictions in their admission. This is not done through any desire to punish the poor and unintelligent, but because they are more frequently subject to the disabilities that prevent admission to America.

Can the Hardships Be Eliminated?

It is true there are many hardships borne by third-class immigrants to America. The question is, Can these hardships be eliminated? Let us take up the more frequent complaints separately. Ellis Island is undoubtedly at times overcrowded. The Harding administration, in keeping with its pre-election promise of economy, has greatly reduced the number of immigrant inspectors at Ellis Island. The capacity of the detention quarters at the island is limited. When these two facts are considered, together with the provision in the immigration law which limits the number of immigrants from each nation and the ruling of the Immigration Bureau dividing this allotment into certain quotas for each month, the main causes of the overcrowding are seen. The refusal of the Immigration Bureau to permit those arriving in the latter part of the month to enter on the quota of the following month caused an intermittent tide of immigration similar to the tides of the ocean. There are many ships on the first of each month waiting beyond the three-mile limit to enter American waters as soon as the clock says that the next month has begun; consequently, Ellis Island is overcrowded at the beginning of each month and practically empty toward its end. Concisely, the crowding is due to too few inspectors and too limited accommodation to handle the periodic influx of immigrants. The aliens stampede the island like a drove of cattle, and the limited immigration force is unable to cope with the condition.

Ellis Island officials speed up the cases of the individual immigrant as fast as possible. Immigrants whose records are clear, who are within their quota and whose health is good, are not kept at the island very long. It is remarkable how quickly the trained inspector can find out whether the individual is admissible, especially so when you remember how involved the immigration law is and how many points concerning the individual's record must be investigated. The inspector makes a record of the immigrant's family and given name, age, sex, marital state, occupation, whether he is able to read and write, and nationality, so as to see whether his quota has been reached. The name and address of the immigrant's nearest relative, whether he has the requisite amount of money required by whom his passage was paid to America, whether he is contract labor, if he expects to make America his permanent home, whether he has a criminal record, the state of his health, if he is apt to become a public charge and whether he is infected with any contagious disease, together with marks of identification for further use by the government, should it later be advisable to deport him—all this must be found out. Immigrants meeting these requirements are admitted within a short time after appearing before the inspector.

Here, however, the possibility of action ceases. Should the immigrant fail to pass on any of these counts, he is detained. Due to the large number of detentions the Special Board of Inquiry before which he must appear is overcrowded and he is forced to undergo the delays, restrictions, inconveniences and humiliations to which Mr. McNeil objects.

Quarters Infested With Vermin

Ellis Island is no Waldorf-Astoria. The sleeping rooms are not above reproach. Its floors are clean, the bedding is sufficient, there is plenty of ventilation and sufficient heat, but the quarters are infested with bugs and roaches and are overcrowded. There is no effort made at selective classification. All races and kinds of people are indiscriminately herded together. The sleeping quarters are about in keeping with the 15- and 25-cent lodging houses on the Bowery, admittedly not very charming surroundings for an educated Englishman temporarily detained as a guest of the American government.

Can these conditions be remedied? The immigrant authorities are evidently doing the best they can under the existing conditions. The blame rests partly on the immigrant. It is incumbent on him to do his part in making living conditions tolerable by the practice of ordinary personal cleanliness. It is a fact that our future citizens, especially those coming from southern Europe, make too infrequent visits to the bathtub. Their person and clothing both are frequently infested with vermin. There is a constant stream of these infected visitors. Their baggage is usually far from being above suspicion and the pestiferous insects have a habit of multiplying rapidly and are intrepid explorers. There is no way to remedy these sanitary evils unless Uncle Sam is willing to be a fairy godfather to all of his

Hardships Third Class Immigrants Have to Bear at Ellis Island

future sons and daughters. He must strip them to the hide, delouse, scrub and disinfect them all, including baggage as well as clothing.

The immigrant authorities genuinely strive to keep the island clean and sanitary, and succeed as far as is possible with the quantity and quality of their guests. The writer is convinced that the detention quarters at Ellis Island are cleaner and more sanitary than were the homes of a majority of the immigrants. In fact, many of them resent the efforts of the officials to interfere with their personal habits. The dining room and other places to which the immigrants do not have continuous access are well kept. The dining room is as clean as the deck of a ship: the floors, walls and tables are spotless, showing evidence of being well scrubbed daily. The food served is wholesome, well prepared and abundant. Here is the bill of fare for one of the days on which the writer visited the island:

Breakfast—Boiled eggs, coffee, bread and butter.
Dinner—Vegetable soup with rice, roast veal, boiled potatoes, pickles, bread and butter, ice cream and coffee.
Supper—Pork and beans, blackberry jelly, bread and butter, tea or coffee.

In addition to this, milk and crackers are served between meals to young children. The quality of the food is good, the eggs are all candled before being cooked. The coffee is strong and of good quality; the bread is baked fresh every day on the island, and the best quality of butter is served. The vegetable soup is not just dish water, but is made from meat stock and contains plenty of vegetables. The roast veal is really delicious. In fact, while there is no great variety, the food served is well prepared, and as good as one would find in the average, middle-class restaurant.

The china, what there is of it, is heavy. The cups have no handles; they might easily serve for small flower pots, but their capacity is great, which is more important than their thinness. Tin plates coated with enamel are used and the table "silver" is—pewter. This is immaterial, for most of the immigrants prefer to eat with their fingers.

There have been many complaints concerning the rough treatment of the immigrants by the inspectors. In order to test the justice of these charges the writer observed the handling of the immigrants, from the moment they stepped off the barge that brought them from the ship until their cases were disposed of. They undergo many hardships and perhaps some unnecessary humiliations, most of which are due to the immigration laws, to the necessity of rushing the individual through the island and to his lack of understanding concerning the machinery of the immigration office.

As to Rough Handling

The inspectors are gruff, which is to be expected. Any small man dressed in a little brief authority becomes dictatorial. Who has not been told by the traffic cop to "Look out where you are driving," or by the train conductor to "Step lively"? These commands, while not couched in pleasing tones, are given in order to expedite travel. It is the same with the immigrant inspectors. They do not handle the immigrant with kid gloves, but they succeed in running him through the mill much more quickly by not stopping to explain the reason for such commands. There are also two sides to the question. While the inspector may be gruff, he is frequently much exasperated by the stupidity of the immigrant and the frantic importunities of his relatives and friends, some of whom will not take "No" for an answer and must be put in their places to prevent the clogging of the immigration machinery.

The guards are callous to human suffering and misery and there is perhaps more of both at Ellis Island than any other place in America. Mothers are parted from sons, husband from wife daily by the inexorable law. Hopes of land in El Dorado, America, leaving behind the old-world miseries, are dashed to the ground by the same power, and the guards show no effect from his human suffering. They remind one of a surgeon in a war hospital who is not moved by the anguish of the wounded soldier brought to the operating table. This does not prevent him from doing all within his power to relieve the patient's suffering. The inspector has not the time or inclination to listen to the tale of woe of each individual. His communication with the immigrants are limited to "Stand here," "Go up there and be quick about it," "Get out of here, you have no business on this floor." These concise commands uttered in no gentle voice, however, hasten the immigrant's departure from the island. While the inspectors pay little regard to the wishes of the individual, he has every opportunity to appeal against injustice. The immigrant officials have assigned commodious quarters to the various immigrant societies, whose agents are given

Hardships Third Class Immigrants Have to Bear at Ellis Island

free access to their fellow countrymen. These agents investigate the case of each immigrant and present it to the government officials before they pass upon his right to admission. His rights are further protected because the inspector cannot order the deportation of an immigrant. It is a one-way street. He can order him freed, but not deported. He must refer all cases which he thinks best to detain to the Immigrant Board, before which body, sitting as a court, each immigrant has the right to appear and, through the aid of an interpreter, present his case. He also has the right of appeal from the judgment of this board to the department in Washington.

Graft is a charge frequently made against the immigration service. There is abundant provocation for graft in the system. The inspector has the power to admit the immigrant into the land of promise. He alone decides whether the immigrant can read sufficiently well to be admitted; whether he has the record of a radical; whether, in a word, he has all the requirements that entitle him to enter America. With his approval, the happy immigrant is shown through the little door that leads to freedom. This arbitrary power is conducive to graft. It is also true that it is impossible to find a large body of men among whose number there are not some who will take a bribe. The amount of graft on Ellis Island, however, is probably very small. The writer was told during his investigations by relatives and friends of the immigrants that graft was very common. In fact, that it was almost impossible to get an alien out without greasing the palms of the inspectors. Close investigation failed to verify these statements. I am not convinced of this fact because of a belief in the extraordinary honesty of the inspectors, but because of the amount of collusion that would be necessary in order to carry out such a scheme.

So that you may understand the difficulties involved, let me explain the modus operandi of the reception and subsequent handling of the immigrants. They are brought from the ship in a greatly overcrowded barge, are received in the reception room by one set of inspectors, who have them examined medically—a very cursory inspection, about a half a minute to a man—and then they are marched upstairs into a vast admission room, almost as large as the Hippodrome, where they are turned over to another set of inspectors, who send them at random into one of the twelve runways, like those through which you pass on going aboard an excursion steamer. An inspector sits at the head of each one of these lines and arbitrarily determines whether the immigrant is immediately admissible or must be detained for further examination. There is no way of telling in advance before which inspector the immigrant will pass. If the inspector in the reception room had been bribed he would have to divide his graft with twelve men, in order to insure that the right man would decide upon a case. Had the immigrant sufficient money to pay this amount of graft one would conclude he would have traveled first-class and thus have avoided Ellis Island. Besides, such a scheme would have to be based on the assumption that all twelve inspectors were crooks.

Opportunity for Graft Small

It is possible that the detained immigrants may by a judicious use of money obtain slight favors during their period of detention, as is done in some American jails, but there is practically no chance for graft, which would lead to the freeing of the immigrant.

How can these inconveniences, discomforts and hardships borne by the immigrants be eliminated?

James J. Davis, Secretary of Labor recommends the following:

By changing the monthly quota system, so as to allow the immigrants arriving at the end of the month to enter on the quota of the following month, thus avoiding the periods of congestion.

By transferring the discretionary power from Washington to the chief of the Immigration Bureau at the entrance port, so that he may decide at once for or against the admission of the individual.

By sending to the various ports in Europe representatives of the Labor Department. These officials to determine whether the prospective immigrants meet all the requirements of the immigration law. If he finds them acceptable he should be empowered to issue a numerically numbered permit to sail to America. No card bearing a number above the quota allowed to that country should be issued. No passport without this numbered card should be vised by the American consul. No steamship company should be allowed to bring passengers to America without such a card under penalty of a heavy fine. It would not be wise to place the entire authority of admitting the alien into the agent's hands, because the immigrant might develop some disease on his trip to America, or new evidence might come up that would bar his admission. Should such aliens passed by him be refused admission at American ports the number of these refusals should be cabled to the foreign agent of the department and a like number of cards of permission be added to the number of allowable admissions for the following month.

Evening Journal (Wilmington, DE)
January 24, 1929

Immigration Law Defended, Also Scored

Darrow Sees Discrimination Against Nordics; Stoddard Sees Benefit

Quips, Puns Keep Crowd Amused

Two Nordics, regarded as intellectual giants by their contemporaries, appeared on the stage of the Shubert Playhouse last night in a verbal joust about Nordics and immigration laws of the United States.

Clarence Darrow, famous criminal lawyer of Chicago, flayed everything on the American scene from Puritans to Elks and Kiwanians. He was decidedly against the closed door immigration policy of the United States and was for more boatloads of immigrants from all parts of Europe, provided the immigrants wanted to come.

Dr. Lothrop Stoddard, a serious-minded sociologist and publicist who proceeded in his support of the Nordic supremacy systematically, argued in favor of the present immigration laws. Mr. Stoddard hails from Boston and is a well-known author and lecturer.

The debate, such as it was, was sponsored by the Kallah, and was in fact the most sensational and most talked of intellectual affair in Wilmington for a long time. Rabbi Louis A. Mischkind, president of the Kallah, presided. The Shubert Playhouse was crowded. Scores of persons were standing.

The subject of the debate was: "Resolved that the present immigration policy of the United States, discriminating in favor of the North European races at the expense of the South European races, is to the best interests of the United States."

Dr. Stoddard launched his views with an immaculate arraignment of the undesirability of the southeastern Europeans in preference to the Nordics. Mr. Darrow fidgeted in his seat all the while. He wrote a stray note or two and then glared into the audience.

Dr. Stoddard asked his opponent and audience to remember that the undesired races did not have customs nor institutions that coincided with American customs and institutions.

When he had finished, Mr. Darrow came to the fore with his wit, satire, irony, and grand array of adjectives and his tendency to stray from the point. He even resorted to punning.

Laughter greeted Mr. Darrow when he asked. "Who are these noble Nordics?" and "In 1620, there landed on Plymouth Rock, a load of Puritans, the most conceited, selfish, narrow-minded, bigoted, self-centered, cruel, mean, contemptible group this country has ever seen."

To Dr. Stoddard, Mr. Darrow's speeches were most witty, flashing, but far from the point at issue. But in the rebuttal, Mr. Darrow continued in his pithy paragraph and the audience seemed to like it. They even got into the habit of applauding almost every other statement he made.

In opening his side of the question, Dr. Stoddard, who is in favor of the immigration law as passed in 1924, said his desire was to deal with the question as it concerns the United States and its people, which he said includes citizens and aliens alike but which is of no concern to the people of other countries. He said that his intention was to discuss theories held by some that the United States belongs to the world and that people should come here and settle as they please.

As against this theory he said that he is opposed to opening the gates of immigration, as that policy would destroy prosperity and lower wage standards and affect the entire life of our people. He cited the stand taken by the American Federation of Labor, which is fighting to have the gates to a flood of immigration kept closed. He then referred to the act of 1924, with its restrictions to the countries of South European races, and said he was in favor of the emigrants of the North European countries because of their higher living standards and their self-preservation, which he termed the first law of the nation, although he said that this word needed analyzing.

He said that the passage of the law was the result of over a half century of the study of problems that the immigration authorities were compelled to deal with. He said restricting immigration that affects the countries of the south of Europe increased living standards in this country, both from an economic and social status, and cited one of the reasons why he was of this opinion: a certain amount of friction develops between the Nordics and the people of the south countries of Europe who have emigrated to this country.

According to Dr. Stoddard, the south and east European countries' immigrants now compose about 14 per cent of the population of this country.

Mr. Darrow, in opening his debate, quoted the law as providing for 150,000 immigrants yearly, and then attacked the makers of this law by dating it back to 1890, and gave as the reason, as he termed it, that the census takers found that the greatest percentage of immigrants to this country up until that time had immigrated from the northern European countries.

Mr. Darrow said the doors of America should be open to everyone who desires to settle here. He said it was unfair to close the doors to the fellows who happened to miss that ship and come over on a later one.

The Pilgrims who came over in the Mayflower in 1620, and landed at Plymouth, did not escape criticism from the lawyer, who characterized them as being so poor that they could not stay at home. Turning to the question of the Indians, he said America was occupied by them at that time, but the Puritans solved this problem, together with generations that sprung up afterwards, by killing them off.

"Why did our ancestors come to America?" he asked, and then answered his own question by replying "to get a better chance," and gave that reason why others are wanting to come to this country.

"I believe all people of the world should be treated alike," he said. "People say we should not have the Sicilians in this country because they rob the rich." Mr. Darrow then became caustic in his remarks regarding the capitalists and the captains of industry by replying "I should worry. Where did they get the money to be robbed of?"

He accused a few in America as dictating to the majority how they should live, how much they should earn, and then concluded this statement by saying if the people of the south and east countries of Europe could aid to better these conditions. "I am for them."

He said that the machine power in the United States is equal to three billion people, and he could not see why the working man today was against having 150,000 foreigners come here every year. Darrow said he has read that the United States is only one quarter settled and if that is the truth, it would be far better off if it was fully settled.

He termed the idea as directed by the Nordics to be a selfish and cruel one and that the United States should harbor more idealism. He said that the immigration law was one of the most unjust the United States ever passed. He expressed the belief that the immigration act with its restrictions came from exaggerated sentiment, worked up as the result of the world war, and like many other laws grew out of super-patriotism. In closing he said there is no such a thing as a race of people, but on the contrary, just a large army of people isolated, for a long period of time, and then vanquished. In rebuttal Dr. Stoddard said that Mr. Darrow's answers were not to the point and that he evaded the question of numerical restrictions. Mr. Darrow in rebuttal argued for a distribution of wealth, and said there is no idealism back of the immigration bill as Dr. Stoddard contends, and his answer to why 85 per cent of the people are poor is due to too much production and not enough distribution, He referred to Prohibition as being one of the greatest plagues ever forced on the country. In closing Dr. Stoddard said he believes in "Keeping America, America," and the problem of immigration is one of the greatest that this country has to deal with. In response to questions during the ten-minute period which was allotted to the audience, both Mr. Darrow and Dr. Stoddard were asked three each. One of these directed to Dr. Stoddard, was: "Prove where immigration has lowered wages and the standards of living", and his reply was in the coal fields of Pennsylvania, which many years ago were inhabited by Cornish, Welsh and Irish, and who later were supplanted by Italians, Hungarians and Slavs.

Honolulu Star-Bulletin
October 3, 1931

Farrington Attacks Stand of McClatchy

Holds Executive Secretary of California Joint Immigration Committee Unsound on Quota for Japanese

 Sharp disagreement with the position of the California Joint Immigration Committee, which opposes extension of the quota system to Japan, is expressed in letters by Wallace R. Farrington, publisher of the Star-Bulletin, to V. S. McClatchy, secretary of the committee.
 The full text of the correspondence, revealing the two points of view on this issue, is as follows:

August 17, 1931.
Mr. V. S. McClatchy, Executive Secretary,
California Joint Immigration Committee,
755 Market Street,
San Francisco, California.

My Dear Mr. McClatchy:

 I have received your letter of January 28th, which seems to be a circular letter sent out to the members of the National Foreign Trade Council to impress upon them your belief that there has been no change of mind among any members of the California Joint Immigration Committee on the subject of extending the ordinary quota to the people of Japan.
 Your letter is an interesting presentation of the length to which some of my good friends and fellow citizens are willing to go in their endeavor to block goodwill and the promotion of commerce and general friendliness throughout the Pacific area.

Weak As Water

I think your presentation of the case is as weak as water. I read it as the nth degree of prejudice and an unwillingness to change with the development of the times.

I believe that the quota law is scientific and sensible exclusion. This makes the exclusion of the Oriental races and peoples entirely unnecessary, and a constant source of needless irritation.

I do not know how long you will be able to block the wheels of progress, but I have no question as to what the American people will eventually do. I mean by that that they will eventually put the people of all nations on a quota basis. This will protect us from any flooding of the country with aliens or unassimilables. It will also keep us on friendly terms with the peoples of all nations, so far as immigration is concerned.

I do not flatter myself that I shall be able to convert you to a normal way of thinking on this subject. I do, however, believe that you have too much good sense to forever continue along the line that you are now moving.

My kindest regards to you and yours.

Sincerely yours,

WALLACE R. FARRINGTON.

McClatchy Replies

September 3, 1931.
Hon. Wallace R. Farrington,
Publisher, Star-Bulletin,
Honolulu, T. H.

Dear Mr. Farrington:

In response to your recent letter criticizing the California Joint Immigration Committee, which represents the state bodies of the American Legion, Federation of Labor and Native Sons of the Golden West, for its opposition to immigration quota for Japan:

Farrington Attacks Stand of McClatchy

You refer to the Joint Committee's attitude as "the nth degree of prejudice" and "an endeavor to block goodwill and promotion of commerce, and general friendliness throughout the Pacific area."

This committee is maintained solely to defend the law excluding aliens ineligible to citizenship. Quota for Japan, or for certain other countries of Asia, would nullify that law; and such quota, therefore, must be opposed by the committee unless its supporting bodies, named above, and their nationals repudiate the policy they have maintained for years.

As concerns the policy itself, the severity of your criticism may be accounted for partly by the wide difference of opinion on the subject of Asiatic immigration, held in Hawaii and California respectively, and by evident lack of information as to the basic reasons which impelled Congress in 1924 to refuse quota to Japan and which still justify California in opposing it.

Hawaii's Labor Policy

Hawaii, in the interest of the plantations, has for many years imported cheap labor from Asia, until today her pure native Hawaiian stock and the whites are entirely submerged, constituting together less than one-seventh of the total population of the territory, while over two-thirds of that total population is Asiatic—Japanese, Filipinos and Chinese predominating. In consequence, for many years, organized labor has given public warning that there is no place for white labor in Hawaii.

While it is claimed that this Asiatic population has been assimilated, testimony on behalf of Hawaii before the House Immigration Committee in 1921 showed that the great strike of plantation employees was in effect a racial conflict in which practically every Japanese on the island of Oahu, regardless of nativity, religion, position or responsibility, and either voluntarily or under duress, took part against the Caucasians by subscription or action. ("America and Japan," J. C. P. 13) Again, within the past few months, Governor Judd vetoed a measure of the Hawaiian legislature petitioning for statehood, and declared that such a request should be postponed until time had shown how the Asiatic majority would exercise its control of the franchise. Still again, during the last campaign an openly declared opposition to Asiatic immigration threatened seriously the re-election of Hawaii's representative in Congress.

Reporting: Immigrants 1803-1931

"Gentlemen's Agreement"

Under the "Gentlemen's Agreement" made by President Roosevelt in 1907 for the express purpose of "preventing the increase of Japanese population in the continental United States," that population increased from about 50,000 in 1907 to about 150,000 in 1920. (Brief J. C. p. 24)

Warned by Hawaii's experience, and regardless of Hawaii's policy and opinion, California sought to protect herself and the mainland against a like fate by opposing the immigration, under any pretext, of all those ineligible to American citizenship, and she forbade by law the intermarriage of whites with any of the colored races, including Filipinos.

Quota for Japan means necessarily quota for other Asiatic races, and each would be entitled to the minimum quota of 100, China and Japan to more. There would thus be admitted annually, under the proposed change, and while the present national origins plan is in force, about one thousand Asiatics of different races ineligible for citizenship. Caucasian Australia has a quota of only 100. It is not, however, so much the actual number admitted as the attendant nullification of a basic principle of the immigration act—the exclusion of all aliens ineligible to citizenship—which California finds most dangerous. This provision is the barrier, non-discriminatory as to particular race or nation, which was erected to protect California and eventually the mainland against possible peaceful invasion of Asiatics—such a one as has inundated Hawaii.

Would Open the Gates

Remove this safeguard and a change in the manner of applying quota might open the gates to Asiatics. For instance, a reversion to the "foreign-born" plan, in force temporarily from 1924 to 1928 (as advocated by some), would admit 2000 Chinese annually; and the not improbable demand from Japan in the future that she be allowed as many immigrants as any other first class power could not be consistently refused if Japanese had been recognized as eligible for immigration. It must be remembered that Japan has declared that quota will not satisfy her permanently and that she must be conceded ultimately full "racial equality"; that is, the same rights and privileges for her nationals, including citizenship, as are conceded to Europeans.

Farrington Attacks Stand of McClatchy

Wallace M. Alexander, whose main business interests are in Hawaii, has organized a committee of 14 to promote quota for Japan. It assumes to represent California sentiment in that direction. The following facts contradict that assumption; first, the practically unanimous action of the state legislature (one opposing vote), which, in 1923, demanded the exclusion of all aliens ineligible to citizenship; and in 1929 opposed quota for Japan, or any modification of the exclusion act; and in 1931 was so deaf to the approaches of the Alexander lobbying committee that the idea of introducing a resolution favoring quota was abandoned. . . . The membership of the three state bodies named above, which maintain this joint committee to oppose quota for "ineligibles" offers a fair cross section of public sentiment.

Others Committed

In addition, the State Grange is similarly committed in opposition to such quota, as is its national body. On July 31, 1931, representatives of the national bodies of the American Legion and the American Federation of Labor appeared before the immigration committee of the U. S. Chamber of Commerce in opposition to quota for Japan.

Equally untrue, and conclusively disproved in a special report to this committee, July 19, 1930, is the statement that a slump in certain branches of our trade with Japan is due to ill will on Japan's part, while it is conceded that the corresponding slump in our trade with other nations is due to general world conditions.

California has only friendship and admiration for the Japanese people. She is selfishly concerned in the maintenance of goodwill and the promotion of commerce on the Pacific. She is not willing, however, to barter state and national welfare for temporary increase in trade, and it is unfair to Japan to suggest that such a condition presents itself in this case. Congress, in 1924, refused to permit the countries of either Europe or Asia to dictate our immigration policy in their own interests; and California feels that Japan, the only country which has continued to find fault with that policy, has no just cause for the dissatisfaction she is encouraged to profess.

It is hoped that the facts herein stated will materially temper your criticism of those who insist that no exception shall be made to the immigration law excluding aliens ineligible for our citizenship. In any event, be assured of my high personal regard.

Sincerely yours,

V. S. McCLATCHY, Exec. Secy.
California Joint Immigration Committee.

Farrington's Reply

September 11, 1931.
Mr. V. S. McClatchy, Executive Secretary,
California Joint Immigration Committee,
785 Market Street,
San Francisco, California.

My Dear Mr. McClatchy:

    I have read with interest your letter of September 3rd, as I read all of your letters with interest and a sympathetic desire to understand your point of view.
    I find nothing in your letter to suggest that I should change my point of view that your attitude represents the nth degree of prejudice, an organized endeavor to block goodwill and to hamper the promotion of commerce and general friendliness throughout the Pacific area.
    You refuse to allow yourself to favorably consider anything but the ancient and to my mind discredited system of shotgun exclusion.
    I consider the quota law to be scientific exclusion, exclusion with sensible adjustment so that all peoples and races may stand on an equality so far as the general laws relate to their entry into our country.
    None of the points that you raise, none of the criticisms that you launch against the population of Hawaii do anything but evidence a desire to throw a smokescreen to cover the blind prejudice that prevails and your refusal to move forward with the natural course of events.

Farrington Attacks Stand of McClatchy

Holding Back Progress

What you are doing is to hold back the progress of the Pacific area, and in that respect the Pacific coast, just as long as it is possible to do so, by stirring up hatreds and bitterness when the situation calls for adjustment and the elimination of the known causes of useless irritation.

When you talk about what you consider the undesirable conditions in Hawaii, you are dealing with a situation that was the outgrowth of the open door in Oriental immigration. We in Hawaii are not worrying about our population, and we are reasonably red blooded Americans. I am willing to present the political activity, the governmental results, the civic standards of our people for comparison with what you can show in San Francisco or the state of California. I doubt if the governor of Hawaii who vetoed the statehood resolution could be elected keeper of the dog pound with his veto as a platform. The legislature, by an overwhelming majority, passed the resolution.

The quota law, adopted as a general national policy, put an end to the open door in all lines of immigration. Thus it eliminated the necessity for the irritating and discriminating exclusion that you and your associates now espouse.

It is when you talk back in this manner that I am more disposed to become convinced that your purpose is to prove an argument rather than to develop a sound, rational and well balanced situation.

Can't Convince Him

As I have said before, I do not expect to convince you, but I do believe that you have too much basic common sense to allow yourself to be continually wandering in the wilderness of a sort of self-hypnosis. When in Peping I listened to the Lama priests of the Orient who vocally grind out the prayers of their order day in and day out until they finally convince themselves that all they say is true.

Your idea of international goodwill appeals to me as on the order of a businessman who deliberately slaps his merchant friends in the face and then smilingly tells them how much he loves them. That for a while until the said merchants get tired of it, and they go elsewhere. You did not work along this line when you were in your newspaper business. I think you will eventually come to see that it is not a sound basis of operation in dealing with the international problems and national problems involved in the control of our immigration on all sides of the continent.

It always pains me when I am unable to agree with you, and I am hoping the day is not far distant when the quota law will be general in its application, and put on the statute books by unanimous consent, including your good self.

Yours cordially.
WALLACE R. FARRINGTON.

For Further Reading

Alba, R. & Nee, V. *Remaking the American Mainstream: Assimilation and Contemporary Immigration.* Cambridge, MA: Harvard University Press, 2003.

Allport, A. *Immigration Policy.* Philadelphia, PA: Chelsea House, 2005.

Bausum, A. *Denied, Detained, Deported: Stories From the Dark Side of American Immigration.* Washington, D.C.: National Geographic, 2009.

Behdad, A. *A Forgetful Nation: On Immigration and Cultural Identity in the United States.* Durham, NC: Duke University Press, 2005.

Briggs, V. M. *Mass Immigration and the National Interest: Policy Directions for the New Century.* Armonk, NY: M.E. Sharpe, 2003.

Brown, W. & Ling, A. (eds.). *Imagining America: Stories from the Promised Land.* New York, NY: Persea Books, 1991.

Chavez, L.R. *The Latino Threat.* Stanford, CA: Stanford University Press, 2008.

Chomsky, A. *"They Take Our Jobs!" And 20 Other Myths About Immigration.* Boston, MA: Beacon Press, 2007.

Cornelius, W., FitzGerald, D., & Fischer, P.L. (eds.). *Mayan Journeys: U.S.-bound Migration From a New Sending Community.* La Jolla, CA: Center for Comparative Immigration Studies, 2007.

Cornelius, W., FitzGerald, D., Lewin, P., & Muse-Orlinoff, L. (eds.). *Mexican Migration and the U.S. Economic Crisis: A Transnational Perspective.* La Jolla, CA: Center for Comparative Immigration Studies, 2010.

Cowart, D. *Trailing Clouds: Immigrant Fiction in Contemporary America.* Ithaca, NY: Cornell University Press, 2006.

Daniels, R. *Guarding the Golden Door: American Immigration Policy and Immigrants since 1882.* New York, NY: Hill and Wang, 2004.

Deaux, K. *To Be an Immigrant.* New York, NY: Russell Sage Foundation, 2006.

DeLaet, D.L. *U.S. Immigration Policy in an Age of Rights.* Westport, CT: Praeger Publishers. 2000.

Delgado, G. *Making the Chinese Mexican: Global Migration, Localism, and Exclusion in the U.S.-Mexico Borderlands.* Stanford, CA: Stanford University Press, 2012.

Delgado, R. J*ustice at War: Civil Liberties and Civil Rights During Times of Crisis.* New York, NY: New York University Press, 2003.

DeSena, J.N., & Shortell, T. (eds.). *The World in Brooklyn: Gentrification, Immigration, and Ethnic Politics in a Global City.* Lanham, MD: Lexington Books, 2012.

Flynn, J.M. *Rescuing Regina: The Battle to Save a Friend From Deportation and Death.* Chicago, IL: Lawrence Hill Books, 2012.

Fry, B.N. *Responding to Immigration.* New York, NY: LFB Scholarly Publishing, 2001.

Gallo, D.R. (Ed.). *First Crossing: Stories About Teen Immigrants.* Cambridge, MA: Candlewick, 2009.

Graham, H.D. *Collision Course: The Strange Convergence of Affirmative Action and Immigration Policy in America.* Oxford, UK: Oxford University Press, 2002.

Groody, D.G. *A Promised Land, A Perilous Journey: Theological Perspectives on Migration.* Notre Dame, IN: University of Notre Dame Press, 2008.

Haerens, M. (ed.). *Opposing Viewpoints: Illegal Immigration.* Detroit, MI: Greenhaven Press, 2006.

Hayes, H. *U.S. Immigration Policy and the Undocumented: Ambivalent Laws, Furtive Lives.* Westport, CT: Praeger, 2001.

Heyer, K.E. *Kinship Across Borders: A Christian Ethic of Immigration.* Washington, D.C.: Georgetown University Press, 2012.

Hing, B.O. *Defining America Through Immigration Policy.* Philadelphia, PA: Temple University Press, 2004.

Hing, B.O. *Deporting Our Souls: Values, Morality, and Immigration Policy.* Cambridge, MA: Cambridge University Press, 2012.

Ho, C.G.T. & Loucky, J. *Humane Migration: Establishing Legitimacy and Rights for Displaced People.* Sterling, VA: Kumarian Press, 2012.

Hochschild, J. Weaver, V. & Burch, T. *Creating a New Racial Order: How Immigration, Multiracialism, Genomics, And the Young can Remake Race in America.* Princeton, NJ: Princeton University Press, 2012.

Hron, M. *Translating Pain: Immigrant Suffering in Literature and Culture.* Toronto, Canada: University of Toronto Press, 2009.

Jacoby, T. *Reinventing the Melting Pot: The New Immigrants and What it Means to be American.* New York, NY: Basic Books, 2004.

Jones Finer, C. *Migration, Immigration, and Social Policy.* Malden, MA: Oxford, 2006.

Kubin, C. E. *Punishing Immigrants: Policy, Politics, and Injustice.* New York, NY: New York University Press, 2012.

Levario, M.A. *Militarizing the Border: When Mexicans Became the Enemy.* College Station. TX: Texas A&M University Press, 2012.

Loucky, J. *Immigration in America Today: An Encyclopedia.* Westport, CT: Greenwood Press, 2006.

Magana, L. *Straddling the Border: Immigration Policy and the INS.* Austin, TX: University of Texas Press, 2003.

Martin, D.A. *Immigration Stories.* New York, NY: Foundation Press, 2005.

Merenstein, B.F. *Immigrants and Modern Racism: Reproducing Inequality.* Boulder, CO: Lynne Rienner Publishers, 2008.

Moloney, D.M. *National Insecurities: Immigrants and U.S. Deportation Policy Since 1882.* Chapel Hill, NC: University of North Carolina Press, 2012.

Motomura, H. *Americans in Waiting: The Lost Story of Immigration and Citizenship in the United States.* New York, NY: Oxford University Press, 2006.

Muller, G.H. *New Strangers in Paradise: The Immigrant Experience and Contemporary American Fiction.* Lexington: University Press of Kentucky, 1999.

Ngai, M. M. *Impossible Subjects: Illegal Aliens and the Making of Modern America.* Princeton, NJ: Princeton University Press, 2004.

Olsen, L. *Made in America: Immigrant Students in our Public Schools.* New York, NY: New Press, 2008.

Park L.S.H. *The Slums of Aspen: Immigrants vs. The Environment in America's Eden.* New York, NY: New York University Press, 2011.

Regan, M. *The Death of Josseline: Immigration Stories from the Arizona Borderlands.* Boston, MA: Beacon Press, 2010.

Riley, J. L. *Let Them In: The Case for Open Borders.* New York, NY: Gotham Books, 2008.

Rose, A. *Showdown in the Sonoran Desert: Religion, Law, and the Immigration Controversy.* Oxford, UK: Oxford University Press, 2012.

Schmidt, R., Alex-Assensoh, Y.M., Aoki, A.L. & Hero, R.E. *Newcomers, Outsiders and Insiders: Immigrants and American Racial Politics in the Early Twenty-first Century.* Ann Arbor, MI: University of Michigan Press, 2010.

Smith, M.P & Bakker, M. *Citizenship Across Borders: The Political Transnationalism of El Migrante.* Ithaca, NY: Cornell University Press, 2008.

St. John, R. *Line in the Sand: A History of the Western U.S.-Mexican Border.* Princeton, NJ: Princeton University Press, 2011.

Suarez-Oroco, A. *Children of Immigration.* Cambridge, MA: Harvard University Press, 2001.

Varsanyi, M. *Taking Local Control: Immigration Policy Activism in U.S. Cities and States.* Stanford, CA: Stanford University Press, 2010.

Watts, J.R. *Immigration Policy and the Challenge of Globalization: Unions and Employers in Unlikely Alliance.* Ithaca, NY: ILR Press, 2002.

Wilkerson, I. *The Warmth of Other Suns: The Epic Story of America's Great Migration.* New York, NY: Random House, 2010.

Wilsher, D. *Immigration Detention: Law, History, Politics.* Cambridge, MA: Cambridge University Press, 2012.

Wong, C. *Lobbying for Inclusion: Rights Politics and the Making of Immigration Policy.* Stanford, CA: Stanford University Press, 2006.

Zolberg, A.R. *A Nation by Design: Immigration Policy in the Fashioning of America.* Cambridge, MA: Harvard University Press, 2006.

Online Resources

George W. Bush Presidential Center: A Nation Built by Immigrants
https://www.bushcenter.org/publications/resources-reports/reports/immigration.

History.com: Immigration History
https://www.history.com/topics/immigration

Immigration Direct: USA Immigration History
https://www.uscitizenship.info/usa-immigration-history/

Migration Policy Institute: US Immigration Trends
https://www.migrationpolicy.org/programs/data-hub/us-immigration-trends

University of Minnesota:
Immigration History Research Center Archives
https://www.lib.umn.edu/ihrca

from
The Archive of American Journalism

Reporting: The Tulsa Riot/1921
ISBN: 978-0-9907137-5-3
List Price: $27.95
On June 1, 1921, an awkward encounter in a small elevator spiraled into the deadliest riot in American history. After two days of burning, looting, killing and mayhem in Tulsa, the reported death toll stood at "unknown (possibly hundreds)" and an entire neighborhood--Tulsa's prospering African-American enclave of Greenwood--had been looted, bombed, and reduced to smoldering ruins.

    Published by The Archive of American Journalism, this collection of contemporary newspaper and magazine articles brings readers a street-level view of the events in Tulsa. The first volume in The Archive's unique Reporting series, it holds up a mirror to the city, its social and economic conflicts, and the wider rifts in American society.

Damon Runyon: Articles/1915
ISBN: 978-0-9907137-8-4
List Price: $12.95
Starting out as a cub reporter in Colorado, Damon Runyon soon found the dusty sandlots of western semi-pro baseball an inadequate field for his major-league writing talent. Moving to New York City in 1910, he landed a beat at William Randolph Hearst's New York American, where he regaled readers with detailed, behind-the scenes tales of famous sportsmen such as Jack Johnson, Jess Willard, Grover Cleveland Alexander ("the Great"), and Babe Ruth. Runyon later moved on to short stories and Broadway plays, but real fascination in his writing can also be found in his clever sketching of talented and sympathetic men, simply climbing into a boxing ring, or trying to hit a small white ball.

    This short collection of articles is the first of a multi-volume edition of Runyon's sportswriting presented by The Archive of American Journalism. Written with wit, insight, and literary flair, the stories have been gleaned from the pages of the Washington Herald, El Paso Herald, Omaha Daily Bee, Richmond Times-Dispatch and other papers. The articles are set out in chronological order, taking the reader through a dramatic year of baseball, boxing, college football, and wrestling from the Classical era of American sports.

Theodore Roosevelt: Wilderness, Vol. 1
ISBN: 978-0-9907137-1-5
List Price: $24.95
In the western states and territories a young Theodore Roosevelt found inspiring loneliness and a hunters' paradise. As "open season" on buffalo, antelope, mountain goat and white-tailed deer brought these species close to extinction, however, he began to understand the meaning and value of conservation—a progression expressed eloquently in the articles he penned for Century, The Outlook and other journals.

Richard Harding Davis: Journalism
ISBN: 978-0-9907137-4-6
List Price: $24.95
The year was 1897, and the place was the front page of Hearst's New York Journal. With "The Death of Adolfo Rodriguez," Richard Harding Davis created a sensation -- and public outrage that helped bring about the Spanish-American War. This collection of 25 original newspaper and magazine stories, complete and unabridged, offers the reader a front page seat to compelling events all over the globe, and newspaper reporting as done with literary skill, social conscience and a flair for the dramatic.

Nellie Bly: Undercover: Reporting for *The New York World* 1887-1894
ISBN: 978-0-9907137-2-2
List Price: $24.95
Nellie Bly's convincing disguises gained her admission to oppressive sweatshops, underground gambling parlors, illicit adoption agencies and creepy mesmerists' parlors, all in the service of sensational headlines and the steadily rising circulation numbers boasted by the New York World. This fascinating collection of original, unabridged articles—compiled for the first time since their original publication--traces Bly's brief yet astounding career as an undercover journalist.

from
historicjournalism.com

"Apparently those in each boat were selected by lot . . .The only other persons originally in my boat were Red Cross nurses of the Post unit and infants. In trampling upon them to safety I foresaw no difficulty.

"But at the dress rehearsal the purser added six dark and dangerous-looking Spaniards. It developed later that by profession they were bull-fighters. Any man who is not afraid of a bull is entitled to respect. But being cast adrift with six did not appeal.

"One could not help wondering what would happen if we ran out of provisions and the bull-fighters grew hungry. I tore up my ticket and planned to swim."

Richard Harding Davis, "President Poincaré Thanks America"
The New York Times, November 6, 1916

"The rumor that a plot is on foot to dope Mr. John Johnson's tea was emphatically denied today by everybody connected with the affair, as it developed that Mr. Johnson does not drink tea. Another rumor that the fight is to be a fake was disproved in no time by your co-respondent, no less a person than Mr. Johnson himself stamping the story as a gross fabrication, wholly unjustified by the facts in the case. Mr. Johnson indignantly declared that he could not possibly lend himself to a cook-up unless the terms of his contract are made more advantageous.

"The champion looks well, and says he is confident as to the outcome of the battle. He confided exclusively to your co-respondent that he anticipates knocking Mr. Willard sub-conscious with a right hand uppercut to the maxilla at half past 4 o'clock in round 12, but he

requests that the public regard this information as strictly confidential until the day after the fight, as it might get back to Mexico and affect the attendance. Mr. Johnson says that up to the knockout it may be a pretty good contest, but he does not want his friends to be too sanguine on that point . . ."
Damon Runyon, "Advance News of the Big Mill"
El Paso Herald, January 20, 1915

"New York Noveletic: Broadway is flooded with ambitious youth. Such were this stage-struck girl and newcomer-wrighter—ambitious in love . . . You can see hundreds of them in New York making park benches their thrones, holding hands in movie balconies or chop-suey joints—walking along the Drive, drinking in the moon and stars—not saying a word—while music runs through their veins and their hearts dance . . . All they hope, pray and hunger for is success. They want life to hug them and make their cheeks bloom . . . Two young people in a strange town finding a home in each other's memory. Well, one day she got a bit part in a show, clicked and was whisked off to Hollywood . . . He went into an ad agency.

"For a while love letters were swapped at a fast clip, then the traffic slowed down, limped along, and finally ceased . . . Love had "taken a powder" . . . A run-out . . . They were riding to the moon on their careers, they couldn't think of anything else. Soon, Christmas cards were their only contact. And now they both have everything they came to New York to get—dreams come true . . . But they are not as happy as they were when they had nothing—except each other."
Walter Winchell, "New York Heartbeat"
Spartanburg Herald, May 3, 1940

"For years and years California's position on the Chinese question has been conspicuously contemptible. We have been imploring Congress to save us from ourselves—to avert from our undeserving heads the consequences of our own selfishness. We have prayed that the Chinese might be kept away from us, in order that we might not hurt ourselves by employing them. Within the past fifteen years I have myself repeatedly submitted, with all due deference, that we need not employ them nor purchase of them if we did not wish, and that we merited no outside assistance so long as we did. Others spoke to the same effect, but we were a feeble and unheeded few.

"All eyes were turned to Washington, all hopes were centered in Congress. It is not surprising that the relief we got was grudgingly given, for our sincerity was open to disproof. If there had been no Congress to help us we should long ago have helped ourselves. But for our own apathy and greed there would not be today enough Chinamen in California to carry a lightweight Polish refugee into the Board of Education."

Ambrose Bierce, "Prattle"
The Wasp, April 3, 1886

"THAT is what it is, a royal sport for the natural kings of earth. The grass grows right down to the water at Waikiki beach, and within fifty feet of the everlasting sea. The trees also grow down to the salty edge of things, and one sits in their shade and looks seaward at a majestic surf thundering in on the beach to one's very feet. Half a mile out, where is the reef, the white-headed combers thrust suddenly skyward out of the placid turquoise-blue and come rolling in to shore. One after another they come, a mile long, with smoking crests, the white battalions of the infinite army of the sea. And one sits and listens to the perpetual roar, and watches the unending procession, and feels tiny and fragile before this tremendous force expressing itself in fury and foam and sound. Indeed, one feels microscopically small, and the thought that one may wrestle with this sea raises in one's imagination a thrill of apprehension, almost of fear.

Flying Through Air

"And suddenly, out there where a big smoker lifts skyward, rising like a sea-god from out of the welter of spume and churning white, on the giddy, toppling, overhanging and downfalling, precarious crest appears the dark head of a man. Swiftly he rises through the rushing white. His black shoulders, his chest, his loins, his limbs—all is abruptly projected on one's vision. Where but the moment before was only the ocean's wide desolation and invincible roar is now a man, erect, full-statured, not struggling frantically in that wild movement, not buried and crushed and buffeted by those mighty monsters, but standing above them all, calm and superb, poised on the giddy summit, his feet buried in the churning foam, the salt smoke rising to his knees, and all the rest of him in the free air and flashing sunlight, and he is flying through the air, flying forward, flying fast as the surge on which he stands. He is a Mercury—a black Mercury. His heels are winged, and in them is the swiftness of the sea. In truth, from out of the sea he has leaped upon the back of the sea, and he is riding the sea that roars and bellows and cannot shake him from its back. But no frantic out-reaching and balancing is his. He is impassive, motionless as a statue carved suddenly by some miracle out of the sea's depth from which he rose. And straight on toward shore he flies on his winged heels and the white crest of the breaker. There is a wild burst of foam, a long, tumultuous, rushing sound as the breaker falls futile and spent on the beach before you; and there, at your feet, steps calmly ashore at Kanaka, burnt black by the tropic sun. Several minutes ago he was a speck a quarter of a mile away. He has "bitted the bull-mouthed breaker" and ridden it in, and the pride in the feat shows in the carriage of his magnificent body as he glances for a moment carelessly at you who sit in the shade of the shore. He is a Kanaka—and more, he is a man, a natural king, a member of the kingly species that has mastered matter and the brutes and lorded it over creation."

Jack London, "The Joys of Surf Riding"
Pall Mall Magazine, September, 1908